PREVIOUSLY ON

F·R·I·E·N·D·S

The Official Companion to Seasons 2 and 3
• PENNY STALLINGS •

BOXTREE

Author's Acknowledgements

Thanks to: Kevin Bright, Adrian Sington, Gina Misiroglu, Emma Mann, Nigel Davies, Grace Ressler, Jamie O'Connor, Lee Kernis, Barry Secunda, Tim Sarkis, Valencia Smith, Alexa Junge, Michael Curtis, Greg Malins, Michael Borkow, Adam Chase, John Shaffner, Michael Lembeck, James Burrows, Phil Gonzales, Shannon Goss, Greg Grande, Richard Padilla, Robert Graff.

First published in 1997 by Boxtree,
an imprint of Macmillan Publishers Ltd, 25 Eccleston Place, London, SW1W 9NF and Basingstoke

Associated companies throughout the world

TM & © Warner Bros. 1997
The FRIENDS trademark is used by Warner Bros. under license from RAMPAGE trading company

10 9 8 7 6 5 4 3 2 1

Friends Production Liaison: Jamie O'Connor

Designed by Nigel Davies

Photo research by Danna Fleishman

ISBN 0 7522 1124 2

Printed and bound by Bath Press

A CIP catalogue record for this book is available from the British Library

Acknowledgments:
pp.38-41 – production design by John Shaffner and Joe Stewart, set decoration by Greg Grande.
pp.28, 51, 75, 107, 132, 146 – costume designs by Debra McGuire.
pp.70-71 – *Friends* CD and cover reprinted by permission. © 1995 Reprise Records.
p.84 – MAD Magazine and all related elements and indicia are trademarks of E. C. Publications, Inc. © 1995. All rights reserved. Used with permission. Artwork by Mort Drucker.
p.95 – letter sent to NBC – reprinted by permission from Marylle Searcey.
p.95 – cartoon – Danziger/© The Christian Science Monitor. All rights reserved.
p.151 – bird invoice – reprinted by permission from Benay Karp, Benay's Bird & Animal Source.

All lyrics on Phoebe songs used by permission. Copyright 1995, 1996 Warner Bros. Music Corp. All rights reserved.

Contents

Introduction

Welcome My Fellow Friends Fanatic,

WHETHER YOU KNOW IT OR NOT, THAT'S WHAT YOU are. How can we tell? You not only bought this book, you're actually reading the introduction. Face it baby, you're hooked. You know *Friends* has something you've never seen on TV before. Characters that think like you and feel like you. It's like they've been watching you as much as you've been watching them.

So, how did *Friends* get that way? To begin with, the show's creators – Marta Kauffman and David Crane along with Kevin S. Bright – had the radical idea of focusing on people in their twenties – a group that, aside from *Baywatch*ers and *Melrose Place*niks, TV seemed to have forgotten. Even more amazing, they got them right. They must have since all of the cast members are routinely accosted on

It takes a village ... the cast and crew of *Friends*.

the street by young fans who tell them how important it is to have a show with their voice and pleading with them not to mess it up! It's hard to think of a show in recent memory that has evoked such passion.

Kauffman and Crane downplay the notion of the show as being demographically oriented. And since the show's weekly audience numbers around 30 million people, they must be right. There aren't that many viewers in their twenties. (Do the math.) But if *Friends*' appeal transcends age, it's because its characters are constantly grappling with the imponderables of life. When not berating themselves for real or imagined blunders, they're tormenting themselves over the deeply mundane details of their lives... weight gains, nose hair, a dirty look from the pizza delivery boy. No character outside a Woody Allen movie has ever agonized so obsessively and so hilariously about anything, everything and nothing at all.

These twentysomethings have every right to be bewildered. They've entered the adult world at a time when the old moral compasses of the past – church, family, community – have gone on the fritz. Instead, their sensibilities have been shaped by *The Brady Bunch* and Watergate – making them at once cynical and naive. They live in a downsized world with far fewer choices than there were for their parents. But that doesn't mean that they aren't going to give it everything they've got – since for all their bawdy talk, they want desperately to make something of themselves, and to do the Right Thing.

By imbuing their creations with so much heart, the show's creators have taken the curse off the popular notion of twentysomethings as passionless slackers. (For half an hour once a week, anyway.) And they've done it without a wisecracking kid, a cop, a boss or even a dog (okay, there's a monkey). There is a wacky neighbor but fortunately he stays out of sight.

Friends was often compared to *Seinfeld* during its first season, with some critics even going so far

She chose *Friends* for her television debut: producers David Crane (left),
Marta Kauffman (middle) **and Kevin Bright** (right) **get loose with *Friends* fan and guest star
Julia Roberts on the set of "The One After The Superbowl".**

as to label it a "*Seinfeld* clone." Boy were they wrong. It's true that their respective characters share a pre-occupation with the trivial, but the *Seinfeld* Four are misanthropes whose misadventures spin into Kafka-esque absurdity. The Friends seem super-real by comparison – even if their stories do unfold via a fusillade of jokes.

That's not to say that *Friends* doesn't have its own surreal moments – such as when Phoebe is possessed by the spirit of an octogenarian named Rose who dies on her massage table (in "The One With The Lesbian Wedding"). In the hands of the *Friends* writers, this incident assumes a Jamesian duality: does Phoebe's temporary derangement spring from deep-seated neuroses dressed up in New Age-y jargon or has the poor thing wandered into an episode of *The X Files*? You won't get any hints from the other Friends – who tend to under-play their reactions to such oddball occurrences in the manner of the characters on the old *Newhart*. The reality lies in the mind of the viewer. The great thing is that however you read it, it's absolutely hysterical.

It takes a Herculean effort to incorporate all these disparate elements into *Friends* and make it

(Above) **"So what if we put a picture frame around the peephole? Nah, too weird." Design maestros Greg Grande and John Shaffner confer on the set.**
(Below) **They make it look easy. Key costumer Nancy Gould and costume designer Debra McGuire.**

They only *look* normal: the *Friends* writers, season three (clockwise from center) – **Marta Kauffman, Adam Chase, Pang-Ni Landrum, Michael Curtis, Seth Kurland, Shana Goldberg-Meehan, Scott Silveri, Michael Borkow, Wil Calhoun, Mark Kunerth, Greg Malins, Ira Ungerleider, Alexa Junge and David Crane.**

The multi-talented Robby Benson directs Courteney Cox in "The One Where Monica And Richard Are Friends".

funny at the same time. So how do they do it? How do the *Friends*' scripts end up so uniformly on the mark, so universal in their appeal, so consistently hilarious week after week? Obvious answer: the writers are, like, geniuses. Sitcom writing is a very peculiar art – and not just any writer can do it. (Remember the stories about F. Scott Fitzgerald's tortured attempts at scriptwriting in Hollywood? If he'd tried to write a sitcom, he'd have drunk himself to death even sooner.) Yes, sitcom writers are different to you and me.

In order to provide you with an idea of what it takes to get to the finish line with each episode of *Friends*, we've tucked anecdotes and bits of show memorabilia – inter-office memos and script pages with the writers' notes – into each installment of the episode guide. (If some of the script pages look a little strange, remember that they come from people who have been sitting around a table till three in the morning trying to think up jokes about silly putty foreskins.) Compare these to the finished product and you'll begin to get a picture of what a long

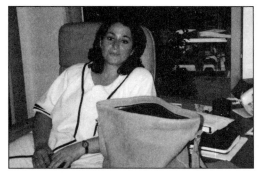

(Above): **Hey, who said you could take a break?** *Friends* **creator Marta Kauffman in an uncharacteristically quiet moment.**
(Above right): *Friends* **writers Adam Chase (with retro hairdo), Mike Sikowitz and Greg Malins.**
(Right): **David Schwimmer waits while props are repositioned during camera blocking for "The One With The Bullies".**
(Below right): **All-round Ace Jamie O'Connor and executive producer Kevin Bright.**
(Bottom right): **David Crane and director James Burrows give notes to the cast on the set of "The One The Morning After".**

strange trip it's been from concept to final draft.

Scattered throughout the guide, you will also find photos from each of the shows of the second and third season along with candid shots displaying cast members and guest stars at work and at play. Here and there you will see a few unfamiliar faces. A general rule of thumb about the last: the people having fun are the producers and actors. The people who look like they're refereeing a wrestling match are the directors. The people with the pained expressions are the writers. The people who look blissfully happy are the set and costume designers. (That's because they get to shop all the time.)

Finally, there are a few little extras – fan mail, an award or two, and the ultimate accolade, a *MAD* Magazine parody – to give you a feel for the constant commotion that has surrounded *Friends* from its inception.

So, now it's time for you to sit back and have as much fun with *Previously on Friends* as we did putting it together.

Penny Stallings

Ross's New Girlfriend

Director:
Michael Lembeck

Writers:
**Jeffrey Astrof
& Mike Sikowitz**

Rachel misses her chance with Ross not once, but twice. She makes up for it by salting his new romance with a number of well-aimed dirty tricks.

BY THIS EPISODE, THINGS HAVE GOTTEN SO CRAZY THAT Phoebe has to explain what's going on at the top of the show. "Ross has been in love with Rachel since forever," she tells us, "but something always got in the way – like cats or Italian guys – so when Ross was away on a dig, Chandler let it slip that Ross was in love with her and Rachel was, like, oh-my-God."

Rachel goes to the airport to tell Ross that she loves him too. But when he comes out of the gate, he's with another woman – who's definitely more than a friend. Rachel is horrified. She tries to scramble through the crowd and ends up crashing over some chairs and cutting her head. Ross can't help but see the commotion. And that Rachel is at the center of it. He doesn't quite understand what she's doing there, but hey, it's great. Oh, and by the way, guys, this is my new, uh, friend Julie.

Back at the apartment, the gang is excitedly awaiting the arrival of the happy couple when Rachel bursts through the door and breathlessly tries to fill them in before he and Julie get there. Julie does her best to ingratiate herself with everyone by telling a funny story, but Rachel steps on the ending. Hard.

The next day at Central Perk, Rachel gets Chandler to ask Ross what went wrong. Ross tells Chandler that he knows now that he was right when he said that there was no way Rachel would ever think of him as anything but a friend. Needless to say, Chandler's version of Ross's answer leaves out that part.

Ross presents Julie for approval.

Feeling humiliated and rejected, Rachel brings bad-boy Paolo home for a little recreational sleeping. Everyone is shocked. (Even the guys.) "How did this happen?" Monica asks incredulously. "I just sort of ran into him," Rachel explains, "in his apartment." Monica gets it and says that if she had a nickel for every guy she, well, if she had a nickel, that's all.

Later, Joey convinces Rachel to tell Ross how she feels about him. She tries, she really does – pulling him out on the roof so they can be alone. But he's too sweet about how she deserves someone who will appreciate how wonderful she is and she's too filled with mixed emotion. She just can't do it.

In the meantime, Chandler goes to Joey's tailor and is shocked when the old man cops a feel while measuring his inseam. "Your tailor is a very bad man," Chandler tells Joey. Give me a break, Joey says, he and his family have been going to this guy for years. "He ran his hand up my leg," Chandler says, "and then there was definite cupping." "Yeah, so?" Joey says. "That's how they do pants." Ross says, right, "in prison!"

Monica has gotten Phoebe to give her a haircut, instructing her to make it look like Demi Moore's.

> **"No, *you* hang up ...**
> **Okay, one, two, three ...**
> **Well, you didn't hang**
> **up either ... Come on,**
> ***you* hang up ... You!"**
>
> *– Ross –*

Unfortunately, Phoebe confuses Demi with Dudley and gives her Dudley Moore's haircut from *Arthur*. So when Phoebe mentions that she's going to cut Julie's hair and that she wants it to look like Andie MacDowell's, that girl from *Four Weddings and a Funeral*, Rachel tells her no, that was *Roddy* McDowall. *Andie* MacDowell is the one in *Planet of the Apes*. Boy, is Phoebe glad she asked!

> **"Your tailor is**
> **a very bad**
> **man. He ran**
> **his hand up**
> **my leg, and**
> **there was**
> **definite**
> **cupping."**
> *– Chandler*

"The One With Ross's New Girlfriend"   Table Draft   7/20/95   37.

(II/P)

JOEY

Look, I can sense when women are depressed
and vulnerable; it's one gifts. My other one is
being able to work the TV remote with my butt.
(OFF HER LOOK) I had a lot of down time this
year. (PUSHING HER TOWARD A CHAIR) Go on.
Sit down.

RACHEL SITS DOWN AND MAKES A MOANING NOISE.

RACHEL

When I saw him get off that plane with her, I
thought that I'd hit rock bottom. But today it's
like there's rock bottom, fifty feet of crap, then me.

JOEY

You've got to tell him.

RACHEL

What about Julie?

JOEY

What about her? Look, I've been with my
share of women – in fact, I've been with
plenty of people's share of women––but
I've never felt about anyone the way Ross
felt about you.

Handwritten notes in right margin:

NOT ANOTHER BUTT JOKE!!

OKAY, how about "work the remote with my nos?"

OH, MUCH BETTER THANKS,

It's not going to get in my way.

What? No butt joke?

— 12 —

THE ONE WITH
The Breast Milk

Director: **Michael Lembeck**

Writers: **Adam Chase & Ira Ungerleider**

The guys face up to a primal aversion to breast milk when Carol nurses Ben in front of them and Monica betrays Rachel by shopping at Bloomingdales with Ross's girlfriend, Julie.

Ross is Mr. Broad-minded about breast-feeding until he discovers that Susan has actually tasted Carol's breast milk.

WHEN CAROL DOES WHAT COMES NATURALLY, casually opening her blouse to nurse Ben in front of Joey and Chandler, they practically jump out of their skins. For starters there's the thing about an actual breast being bared … right in front of them! And then there's the whole yucky idea of the sucking and the bodily fluids. Ross can't believe they're so freaked out by something so natural, so beautiful. Determined to make this a learning experience he makes them ask Carol questions about the process. Joey asks, if the baby blows in one, will the other get bigger?

The next day at the coffeehouse, Ross's new girlfriend Julie says she knows someone at Bloomingdales who can get them a discount and is anybody interested. Monica is definitely in – until Chandler warns her that that would be like cheating

For MICHAEL LEMBECK   A.M. P.M.

Date_____ Time_____

WHILE YOU WERE OUT

M DAVID CRANE

Of_____

Phone_____

Fax_____

Mobile_____ Area Code Number Extension

	PLEASE CALL
TELEPHONED	WILL CALL AGAIN
CAME TO SEE YOU	URGENT
WANTS TO SEE YOU	SPECIAL ATTENTION
RETURNED YOUR CALL	

Message STANDARDS ASKS THAT YOU USE CAUTION WHEN SHOOTING THE BREAST-FEEDING SCENE

Signed_____

Oh like I didn't know that ML.

The victorious Joey ends up walking into a cardboard sunset with a mighty purty little blonde gal from cosmetics named Annabel.

The next day, Monica comes into Central Perk loaded down with shopping bags from Bloomies and tells Phoebe to cover for her with Rachel. This ploy goes as well as you would expect – which is not very well at all. But Rachel doesn't really catch on till she finds a receipt for Monica and Julie's lunch. Monica says someone must have stolen her credit card. And Rachel asks if that person also put the lunch receipt in her pocket. Monica breaks down and admits her deceit, but assures Rachel that it didn't mean anything to her and she was thinking of Rachel the whole time.

Hard as she tries, which is not very hard, Rachel can't put Monica's infidelity out of her mind. It's bad enough that that bitch Julie has stolen the person she's supposed to be with, but now she's stealing Monica. "No one can steal me from you," Monica tearfully tells her. She wishes it hadn't turned out this way, but Julie is her brother's girlfriend. Can't Rachel just try to get to know her, Monica pleads, for her sake?

Phoebe tells Carol that Ross was repulsed when she tasted the breast milk she left for Ben. Yeah, Ross says, so? Susan casually comments that it tastes sweet, like cantaloupe juice. Ross is boggled and not a little grossed out. "You mean you've tasted it?" he shrieks. That's exactly what she means.

on Rachel in her house of worship. She knows he's right. She'll just have to get out of it. But then when Ross gives her an extra special thank you for being nice to his new girlfriend, there's no way she can back out.

Joey has a part-time job as a perfume spritzer in the men's department of a mid-town store. Things are fine till a mysterious stranger – in shiny black cowboy duds with a husky Clint Eastwood voice – rides on to the floor packing a rival perfume spray. The Hombre Man is such a hit that the store makes Joey Hombre Man Number Two. But it quickly becomes clear that this town isn't big enough for both of them. They have a shootout and the man in black ends up spraying a little old man in the eye.

"And then, oh, one thing led to another, and before I knew it, we were ... shopping. But we only did it once. And it didn't mean anything to me. Really. I was thinking of you the whole time."
– Monica

THE ONE WHERE
Heckles Dies

Director: **Kevin S. Bright**
Writers: **Michael Curtis & Gregory Malins**

Mr. Heckles, Rachel and Monica's weird downstairs neighbor, dies and leaves them all his junk; Chandler sees the ghost of Chandler Future in Mr. Heckles' pathetic remains.

CHANDLER ANNOUNCES THAT HE HAS BROKEN UP with Joan, the girl with the big nostrils. As usual, Rachel, Monica and Phoebe are dismayed by the guys' superficiality when it comes to women. They try to defend her, saying how sweet she is. Chandler acknowledges that, yeah, she is nice and everything, but the nostril situation was out of control. Like, when she sneezed, bats flew out of her nose! And when she leaned back, he could see her brains. Joey says he's got to side with Chandler on this one, seeing as how there are certain physical characteristics you just can't get past. Take that girl with the really big Adam's apple he dated when he first moved to the city. The gang looks at him in disbelief. "Joey, women don't have Adam's apples," Ross tells him gently. "You guys are messing with me, right?" Joey says nervously. They're not, of course, but it's just too cruel. They let it pass.

Their conversation is interrupted by a knock at the door. It's weird Mr. Heckles from downstairs. He accuses them of stomping around and disturbing his birds. What is he talking about? They haven't been stomping. And he doesn't have any birds! Not more than a few seconds later, he bangs on the ceiling for quiet. Well, if he's going to bang, then they'll just stomp. He bangs again. They stomp again. Him. Them. Then, nothing, only silence. But then there would be, seeing as Mr. Heckles has dropped dead.

Mr. Heckles may be gone, but he's not through with Monica and Rachel. In his will he has left all his

> **"When I first moved to the city, I went out a couple of times with this girl – really hot, great kisser – but she had the biggest Adam's apple. Drove me nuts."**
> *– Joey*

> **Check out Kevin Bright's nephew, Noel Bright** (third from right) **and writer Michael Curtis** (far right) **making guest appearances. "He must've been sweeping. They found a broom in his hand. It coulda been me."**
> *– The Super*

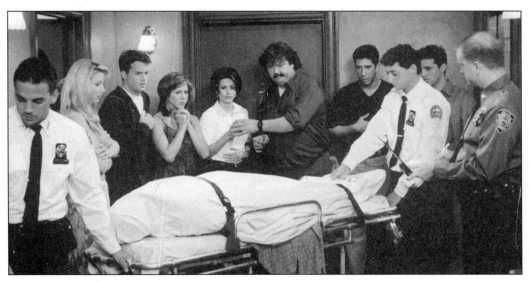

"The One Where Heckles' Dies" Pre-Table Draft 7/28/95

CHANDLER (CONT'D)

You figure "I'm single now, but I won't be later." But what if I <u>never</u> find anybody? Or even worse, what if I've <u>already</u> found the right woman but dumped her 'cause... 'cause she pronounces it "supposebly".

I think all this stuff hits a little too close to home for some people

JOEY

Chandler, come on. You're gonna find somebody.

CHANDLER

How do you <u>know</u> that? How??

JOEY

I don't know. I'm just trying to help here, man.

CHANDLER

You'll see. You guys are all going to go on and get married, while I'm still living alone in our cruddy apartment -- which, because it's rent controlled, I'll never leave... Promise me something, Joey. When you're married, can I come over to your house for the holidays?

MAN, IF I HAVE TO EAT ONE MORE CHICKEN CESAR SALAD, I THINK I'M GONNA (KILL SOMEONE)

WOULD A JOB IN ADVERTISING BE SO BAD?

I WISH I COULD DRAW

Bright Kauffman Crane

KEVIN'S SCHEDULE

7:30 AM DENTIST APPOINTMENT W/ DR. BARRY SCHAFFER
9:00 AM PRODUCTION MEETING - EPISODE #257
10:00 AM TABLE READ - EPISODE #257
11:00 AM CASTING
12:00 PM CAMERA BLOCKING - EPISODE #256
1:30 PM LUNCH WITH KIRSTIE ALLEY
2:30 PM CONTINUE CAMERA BLOCKING - EPISODE #256
4:30 PM EDIT EPISODE #255
6:00 PM PARENT TEACHER CONF. @ VILLAGE SCHOOL
8:00 PM DINNER WITH MARTA & DAVID
9:00PM-12AM MIX EPISODE #253

worldly possessions to the "noisy girls in the upstairs apartment." Apparently, poor Mr. Heckles didn't have any family – or friends – on whom to inflict his junk heap of a life.

Among the debris, the guys find Mr. Heckles' Big Book of Grievances. Joey is proud that he's gotten a mention until he sees that it's something about his bringing home a drag queen. And what's this? Hey, it's Mr. Heckles' high school yearbook! This oughta be good. They look up his picture. Not only does he look pretty normal, he was class clown! Chandler begins to realize to his horror that the two of them have a lot in common. Look at his crabby scribblings on the women he dated; no woman was good enough for him either! Chandler has seen the Ghost of Chandler Future and he's chilled down to his crew socks. He rushes out to call (oh-my-god) Janice.

"You always assume you're going to find somebody. But what if I never find anybody? Or even worse, what if I've already found the right woman but dumped her 'cause ... 'cause she pronounces it supposebly?"

– Chandler –

The next day at Central Perk Janice walks in – big as a house. No, she's not fat; she's pregnant. "You *wish*, Chandler Bing," she hoots when he timorously asks if it's his. "You couldn't have told me about this over the phone?" he asks her. "What, and miss your face? Oh no. Janice likes to have her fun."

Fortunately, Chandler has his (women) friends to counsel him. "You are *not* a freak. You're a guy!" they tell him. "You are no different than the rest of them." Actually, he might even be better. "You're ready to take risks," Monica encourages him. "You're ready to be vulnerable. You are ready to make a commitment!" Chandler thinks this last one might be going a little too far. Even so, he's dead set on showing them – and himself – that he's a new man. And he is. In a way. And to prove it, he asks Allison at work for a date, even though she's got an unusually large head.

Phoebe's Husband

Director:
Gail Mancuso

Writer:
Alexa Junge

The gang discovers to its collective amazement that Phoebe has been married. But they all have secrets as it turns out – including the fact that, as Ross confides to Rachel, he and Julie haven't had "The Sex."

(Right) **Lisa Kudrow and guest star Steve Zahn.** (Below) **See, they don't really hate each other. Jennifer Aniston and Lauren Tom schmooze during a rehearsal break.**

RACHEL IS ON THE PHONE WITH HER MOTHER, assuring her that New York isn't all that dangerous, when a strange man strolls through the door. Fortunately, he isn't a serial killer or anything. He's Duncan, Phoebe's husband. *Phoebe's husband!?*

Your friends don't always know everything about you. Even your best friends. Like, for instance, Monica had no idea that Phoebe had been married to Duncan – even though they were room-mates at the time. She never told Monica because she was sure she'd be judgmental. "Of course, I wouldn't approve!" Monica raves. "I mean you were totally in love with this guy, who was – hello? – gay." It's not like it's any big deal, Phoebe says, she was just helping him get his green card. Monica reminds her that she was so depressed when he left town she stayed in her pyjamas for a month.

As it turns out, all the gang has secrets. Like that time Monica's underwear ended up on a telephone pole after a hot night with Fun Bobby. And then there's Joey's porno movie. Oh, and how about Chandler's third nipple? Actually Joey knew about this one, although he thought it was just a "nubbin" – like Chandler told him. The next day at the coffee-house, Julie tells Chandler that in some cultures a third nipple is a sign of virility; and that whoever

REGARDING JOEY'S PORN MOVIE.

"Comedy writers (at least the ones on this staff) enjoy coming up with titles for porn movies. (Some comedy writers keep an ongoing list that they update and add to.) Originally, the title of Joey's porn movie was 'How to Suck Seed in Business' but the network found this a little Over the Line. All week long, titles were pitched ('Casa-Spanka', 'Mystic Penis', 'Breakfast Chub', etc.) but, ultimately, none were used."

ALEXA JUNGE

has one gets the best hut and the women dance naked around them. Naturally Chandler wants to know if any of these cultures are in the tri-state area.

After Julie leaves, Ross asks Rachel what's the longest time she's been in a relationship without having "The Sex" – because technically he and Julie aren't. Rachel is not unhappy to hear this and proceeds to counsel him in ways guaranteed to make things worse, assuring him that there is nothing sexier to a woman than a guy who doesn't want to have sex.

Across town at Madison Square Garden, Phoebe is visiting Duncan backstage at the Ice Capades – where he is an ice dancer. She tries to be cool, but it's clear that she still likes this guy. A lot. So what if he's gay? But Duncan has some news. He's not gay! In fact, the reason he's popped up in Phoebe's life again is because he's getting married and he wants a divorce. Phoebe can't believe it: after all, he's so smart and funny and he throws such great Academy Award parties. He thought he was gay too. "But now I know I don't have a choice about this," he says. "I was born this way." Phoebe wonders if things would've been different between them if he'd figured this stuff out sooner. He tells her he loves her – which is a very good answer.

In the meantime, Ross has decided not to go with Rachel's waiting-on-the-sex-

thing. So, more than likely, he confides to Rachel, he and Julie are going to have sex tonight. As soon as they watch Joey's porno film – which Chandler, stand-up pal that he is – has managed to dig up. Everybody is psyched to see it. Even Joey. But that's probably because he doesn't actually take his clothes off.

"Oh! I have to get over it. I didn't realize that. I have to get over it. I'm just going to have to write that on my hand."

– Rachel –

sarcastically responding to advice that she "get over" Ross dating Julie.

Ross and Julie say goodnight, but then Rachel suddenly decides that now is the time to get to know Julie. In depth. The incredibly long story of Julie's life ends up putting the others to sleep, so it's very late by the time Ross and Julie are ready to leave. Rachel pulls Ross aside and asks him if he's still gonna, you know…? Ross says, yes, definitely.

Five Steaks And An Eggplant

Director:
Ellen Gittelsohn

Writer:
Chris Brown

In "Five Steaks And An Eggplant," the Friends split up into Haves and Have-nots for the first time.

"You're going to sneeze on my fish, aren't you?"
– Chandler

Cue waiter alert: producer David Crane's cousin, Spencer Cherashore.

ROSS IS STILL GOING HOT AND HEAVY WITH JULIE WHO'S off in New Mexico on a dig. He misses her and that reminds Chandler that he misses having someone to miss. And then, as if in response to a sitcom prayer, he overhears his answering machine recording a message from a certain sexy-sounding Jane. This Jane is trying to track down an old boyfriend named Bob in the hope that they might get back together. Chandler continues to eavesdrop until Jane happens to mention that she's a little drunk, and, well, naked. He dives for the phone and begins to talk to her as (of course) Bob. "So what have you been up to?" he asks. You know, teaching aerobics, oh and by the way, she says, those *are* her legs on the new James Bond poster. Chandler makes a date to meet her at Central Perk tomorrow around "five-ish." Sure, it's going to be a little tricky, but he'll figure it out then.

In the meantime, Ross's birthday is coming up and Chandler wants everybody to chip in $62 for a gift. No problem, Joey says, he'll just sell a kidney. That price tag is a little steep for Rachel and Phoebe too. As so often happens with groups of friends with differing incomes, tensions escalate into bad feelings. What should have been a fun night on the town fizzles into a major mope.

Hoping to smooth things over the next day, Monica brings home the makings for a great, at-home meal: five steaks for the guys and an eggplant for Phoebe. The steaks were a thankyou from a grateful distributor. And that's not all, Ross says. Check out six tickets for the Hootie and the Blowfish concert and it's their treat! Nice gesture, but it just makes Joey feel even more like a charity case. Ditto Phoebe and Rachel.

"The day after" finds Chandler in all his glory. "I had sex today," he crows to Ross. "I was awesome. She was biting her lip to keep from screaming." As if on command, Jane calls his answering machine again looking for Bob. Doing his macho Bob voice, Chandler picks up the phone. She tells him she met a new guy and even had sex with him two hours ago. "Oh really," says Chandler, "and how was it?" "Nothing compared to you," she tells him. "I had to keep biting my lip to keep from calling out your name."

Monica, Ross and Chandler guiltily go off to the Hootie concert without the other guys. Just one song, and then they'll split. But they're still there an hour later, when a guy Monica used to baby-sit comes over to say hello. It's Little Stevie Fisher and he's all grown up and a lawyer for the band. He offers to take them backstage!

The following morning, Phoebe notices that Monica has a hickey. Oh that, Monica says, I fell down. "On someone's lips?" Rachel asks. Monica admits that she got it from a Blowfish at the, well, party after the show. "You partied with the Blowfish?" Phoebe whimpers. "Don't blame us," Ross says, "You coulda been there too." Suddenly, Monica gets a page from her boss. She's been fired for accepting those steaks that no one wanted anyway. Now she not only has a very conspicuous hickey, but she's broke and out of a job, too.

"I'm trying this new screening thing. I feel like if I'm always answering the phone, people will think I don't have a life."
– Chandler

Chandler, Ross and Monica overcome their guilt feelings, and stay till the end of the Hootie and the Blowfish concert.

The Baby On The Bus

Director:
Gail Mancuso

Writer:
Betsy Borns

Joey and Chandler leave Ben on a city bus while using him as bait to get girls, and Phoebe is fired from her singing gig at Central Perk, even though she does it for free.

MONICA IS CRAZY ABOUT ROSS'S BABY SON BEN, BUT every time she picks him up he starts to cry. Does he hate her? Don't be silly, Ross assures her, he'll come around. After all, she spends so much time with him she's practically his second – or anyway – third mother. However, when Ross has to go to the hospital following an allergic reaction to her kiwi lime pie, he has no choice but to leave Ben with the world's two most unlikely nursemaids – Chandler and Joey. But they couldn't be happier. And the reason is simple. Everybody knows women are suckers for babies. If they hit the street with Ben in tow, they'll have to beat them off with a stick. And in fact, they do attract a stunner (guest star, Lea Thompson) right off the mark. The only problem is she thinks they're gay.

Meanwhile, downstairs at Central Perk, Phoebe is doing a particularly abstract number about singing in the shower and how Tegrin spelled backward is "Nirget" when the boss calls Rachel over and tells her he can't take it anymore – he's got to fire Phoebe. Make that *Rachel* has got to fire Phoebe – now – because he's already got a new girl coming in to take her place. Naturally, Phoebe is devastated – particularly when she hears that her replacement is actually going to get paid. Okay, well, she'll just go back to singing on the street. On the street right outside Central Perk's window. Loudly.

Across town, Chandler and Joey's next encounter with the opposite sex is going a little better. They follow two hot-looking girls on to the bus, and spout off randomly about how they are

"Here's the deal: we lost a car seat on a bus today. It was white plastic with a handle, and it fits on to a stroller. Oh. And there was a baby in it."

– Joey

definitely heterosexuals. Pleased with their progress, they then follow the hot-looking girls off the bus until they suddenly realize they've left Ben behind. They chase the bus down the street screaming at the top of their lungs, and we all know how much good that does. Especially in New York. On the verge of hysteria, they call the Transit Authority and ask what would happen if someone really stupid left a baby seat on the bus – with the baby in it? What a coincidence, they're told, someone has done just that. Fortunately, the baby is safe and sound and ready to be picked up. And that's exactly what the guys would do, if only they could remember what Ben looks like – because, see, two boy babies, the same age and the same size, got left on buses today by really stupid people. So they do what any two rational human beings would do. They flip a coin.

Down in the Village, Phoebe has been at it for hours but she's only earned $8.27. And really not even that, seeing as how she put in the first two dollars herself. What hurts her most is that her signature song, "Smelly Cat", only brought in a quarter and a condom. She's feeling pretty low by the time she has an encounter with Stephanie, the new singer, who is played by guest star Chrissie Hynde. (No wonder she's getting paid.) Phoebe gamely challenges her expertise, asking her how many chords she knows ("all of them") and whether her guitar has a strap (it doesn't, but huh?). It gets edgy for a second, but happily the two troubadours end up bonding and even sing a duet of "Smelly Cat".

Back home, Monica and Ross have just returned from the hospital when Chandler and Joey slink in the door carrying, well, a baby. The guys go numb when Monica picks it up and it doesn't cry. Then they practically collapse with relief when it quickly starts to wail. Ross just wants to know one thing though: how come Ben's diaper says "Property of Human Services"?

Phoebe asks Stephanie (guest star Chrissie Hynde) how many chords she knows.

THE ONE WHERE

Ross Finds Out

Director:
Peter Bonerz

Writer:
Michael Borkow

Ross and Julie are starting to get serious until Rachel leaves Ross a drunken answerphone message that reveals her true feelings.

"Five more ... and I'll flash you."
– *Monica*

CHANDLER HAS BEEN FEELING PARTICULARLY repellant to women of late. Phoebe assures him that he's adorable even if he has put on a little weight, er, insulation. But this boy's in luck because Monica, who just happens to be in dire need of a project, would love to remake him. But Chandler is afraid that the exercise thing will interfere with his all-important lying-around time. He finally gives in, but Monica definitely has her work cut out for her. For one thing, Chandler has a tendency to jog in the other direction and hail a cab for home. And he won't do his sit-ups unless she promises to flash him.

Phoebe's having problems with the opposite sex too. She tells Joey that her new boyfriend Scott doesn't want to have sex with her. Joey gently suggests that maybe he likes to, you know, drive on the other side of the road. Phoebe is sure that's not it because he's not British. No, Joey tries again, "Maybe he's gay." But Phoebe felt something – literally – when they were dancing that makes her certain he's not.

Rachel makes a big show of being over Ross. What choice does she have? It looks pretty serious between him and Julie. They're even getting a cat. But that's okay, because Rachel is moving on too. In fact, as she announces to everyone in Central Perk, she has a date tonight herself. With a man!

Luckily that man, Michael (guest star Arle Gross), is a sweetheart. He does his best to connect with Rachel, even though he is trying to get over a divorce himself. But all Rachel can talk about is this guy she knows and how he and his new girlfriend

"She's insane, the woman is insane. It's before work. It's after work. During work, she has me doing butt clenches at my desk, and now, they won't bring me my mail anymore."
– *Chandler* –

Rachel's blind date Michael tells her he's not having *such* a bad time with her. But that's only because he's been replaying *Diner* in his head for most of the evening.

are getting a cat. Michael assures her she'll feel better as soon as she gets some closure. Rachel thinks this closure concept is brilliant. (She would probably think that about anything, since by this point she's pretty blotto.) She pesters the guy sitting at the table behind her into giving her his cellular phone so she can call Ross and tell him that she's finally over him. Fortunately, he's not home. Unfortunately, she leaves a message on his answering machine.

The next morning Ross shows up at the apartment to pick up some cat toys. Rachel, who has a hangover and only a vague memory of the night before, asks him if they spoke on the phone last night. Ross says no, he slept at Julie's, but that reminds him that he needs to check his messages. The fatal phone call suddenly flashes through Rachel's mind. She jumps on Ross's head (literally) and rides him across the room to keep him from making the call. Too late. He heard and he wants to know just what this Over Him thing is all about. He finally gets it but it's too huge to even contemplate. After all, he's got a girlfriend. And a cat.

In the meantime, Phoebe has decided that Scott doesn't want to sleep with her because she's not sexy. Joey hates her dumping on herself, and tells her how when he first saw her he said to Ross, "Excellent butt, great rack." Phoebe is "officially offended" but unofficially thrilled.

She finally confronts Scott who explains that the reason he hasn't gotten into the sex thing with her is because sex can be a very emotional thing for a woman and he wanted to hold off till he was really serious. So she tells him to Relax Please and just enjoy it. Joey says, "You mean to tell me that he got you to *beg* to sleep with him? This man is my god!"

**It finally happens ...
the much anticipated kiss.**

Later Rachel is locking up at Central Perk when Ross shows up unannounced. Ross says that even though he's loved her since the 9th grade, it's too late. The ship has sailed. "The point is I don't need this now," he asserts. Rachel doesn't need it either. He slams out of the door. But when he looks back, he sees that Rachel has dissolved into tears. He's back in a flash (after Rachel wrestles the locks open) and they kiss deeply and for real.

Jennifer Aniston

"You know that Martian guy in the Bugs Bunny cartoon, the real big monster with the red hair? I used to think I looked like him."

Jennifer Aniston

JENNIFER ANISTON IS THE ONE, ALL RIGHT. THE GIRL of the moment. The face that sells hundreds of thousands of magazines all over the world – whether there's an actual interview on the inside or not. She's the one with the child-woman appeal – the seasoned professional who sometimes looks like a little girl playing dress-up in her mother's clothes. She's the reigning paradigm of beauty – the regular-looking girl you might not look at twice if you saw her on the street. She's all of these things and more. But then again, maybe not.

> *"I was somebody who never loved my hair. So it was sort of ironic to all of a sudden have this hair be a fad."*
>
> JENNIFER ANISTON

The truth is Jennifer Aniston is very much in the process of becoming. Stardom overtook her at the tender age of 25. And yet it would be inaccurate to say that the she wasn't prepared. By that point, Jennifer had been working at and studying her trade for more than half of her life. Born in 1969 in Sherman Oaks, California, Jennifer spent a year of her childhood living in Greece. Her family then relocated to New York City. Her parents

After all these years, she's willing but he's not. Will Rachel and Ross ever work things out?

divorced when she was nine and Jennifer remained with her mother. Her reaction to the split sounds very much like that of Rachel's upon hearing that her parents were breaking up: "It was awful," she has said. "I felt so totally responsible. It's so clichéd, but I really felt it was because I wasn't a good enough kid."

However powerful her feelings of guilt about the split might have been, no emotion could compare to her deep-rooted desire to be a star. And then too, acting was the family business. Her mother Nancy was a sometime model and actress and her father John Aniston played the long-running role of villain Victor Kiriakis on *Days of Our Lives*. Even her godfather was a household name – her dad's good friend and fellow Greek, actor Telly Savalas. It's not surprising then that even as a child of twelve, Jennifer knew she wanted to take up permanent residence in the land of make-believe. "I remember dreaming about it, about being on TV." Her resolve grew even stronger after seeing *Children of a Lesser God* on Broadway. "I was sitting in the second or third row," she recalls, "and I was just so blown away, and I walked out saying, 'That's what I want to do.'" She pursued her dream despite her father's objections. "Well, I wasn't terribly thrilled," he has been quoted as saying. "I don't think any father who knows anything about this business would be thrilled to have a daughter in it." But what

> "Jennifer is without a doubt the worst driver in the world. Just knowing that she is out for the evening is enough to make me stay home."
>
> MATTHEW PERRY

The original résumé and head shot that got Jennifer Aniston her first audition for a new television comedy called *Friends Like Us*.

JENNIFER ANISTON

TELEVISION
BURKE'S LAW - Guest Star - Spelling/CBS
MUDDLING THROUGH - Columbia/CBS Pilot
QUANTUM LEAP - Universal/NBC
THE EDGE - Series Regular - TriStar/Fox Network
HERMAN'S HEAD - Guest Star - Fox

SUNDAY FUNNIES - Series Regular - NBC
FERRIS BUELLER - Series Regular - NBC
MOLLOY - Series Regular - Fox

THEATRE
FOR DEAR LIFE - "Emily" - N.Y. Shakespeare Festival - Public Theatre
DANCING ON CHECKERS GRAVE - "Lisa" - Second Story Theatre - NYC

TRAINING
Ellen Burstyn - Master Class - LA
Anthony Abeson - Theatre Works - NYC
High School of Performing Arts - Drama '85-'87 - NYC

Friends costume designer Debra McGuire designed Rachel's wardrobe for a newly independent young woman who's given up her daddy's charge card, but not her passion for clothes.

Costume design by Debra McGuire

John Aniston didn't realize then was how tough and determined his little girl was. "I wanted her to go to college, and she just didn't want to," he says. "She was anxious to get on with it. Once she decided what she wanted to do, she was very driven."

Jennifer began her professional training as a drama student at Manhattan's High School of the Performing Arts, better known as the *Fame* school. She continued to live at home after graduating in 1987. Her days were spent auditioning, and her nights waitressing at a well-known hamburger joint called Jackson Hole. She appeared in several off-Broadway productions before deciding to move to California where the real action was. There she covered expenses with a telemarketing job. Although she was struggling, she looks back on that period with a kind of bittersweet longing: "You always miss parts of your past," she says. "Back then it was familiar and safe, and now you have no idea what's around the corner." In 1989, Aniston landed her first television role, as a series regular on *Molloy*. She also appeared in *The Edge*, *Ferris Bueller* and *Herman's Head*. By this point, she was living in LA's hillside community of Laurel Canyon with a tight-knit group of struggling actors and writers – who remain her close friends today. Although she worked steadily for five years, the reality was that she was

"She *was* the part," says producer Kevin Bright of Jennifer Aniston (caught here during a rehearsal break for "The One Where No One's Ready"). "She was funny. She was pretty. It all came through in one big stroke."

basically floundering until her agent finally told her that the reason she was not being taken more seriously was that she was overweight. "My agent gave it to me straight," she says now. "Nicest thing he ever did … the disgusting thing of Hollywood – I wasn't getting lots of jobs 'cause I was too heavy." Jennifer was forced to face the hard reality that if an actor's outer shell isn't pleasing to the Hollywood's powers-that-be, chances are they won't bother to probe deeper in search of talent. Hearing the message loud and clear, Jennifer set out to shed thirty pounds off her five-foot five-inch frame. "It was amazing to see this thing emerge," she says of her post-diet and exercise figure. "I never knew I had this body in me." It was that sleeker, leaner body that auditioned for a much talked-about new series called *Friends*. Originally Jennifer was asked to read for the role of Monica, but she demanded instead to audition for the part of Rachel Green, the suburban princess-turned-coffeehouse waitress. "It happened so fast," she has said. "I went in, read the script, laughed out loud, got home and an hour later had the part." The show's producers Marta Kauffman, David Crane, and Kevin Bright knew immediately they had found their Rachel. "She *was* the part," producer Kevin Bright says admiringly. "She was funny. She was pretty. It all came through in one big stroke."

Aniston, now a seasoned veteran of the sitcom wars, knew right from the start that *Friends* was going to be different, that it wouldn't be another short-lived involvement. "It's all about relationships," she says of the show. "And people really need to see something that they can relate to – real life situations." It was character-driven comedy, something at which, it turns out, Jennifer Aniston excelled – and on occasion even dominated. In the process she gained her own devoted following – something to be admired since she did so while playing a ditzy, spoiled waitress who's a little on the bitchy side.

And now it can rightfully be said that Jennifer Aniston is a bona fide movie star – in light of the

box office and critical success of l997's *Picture Perfect*. Some are even saying that she is poised to take Sandra Bullock's place as America's big screen sweetheart. But that is no random stroke of luck either. Aniston was the first of the *Friends* cast to juggle film work while shooting the series, playing small roles in *Till There Was You* and *She's the One* – which she shot for director Edward Burns (*The Brothers McMullen*) on her weekends off from *Friends*. And as for *Picture Perfect*, it was a project she herself set in motion after her dad slipped her the script – co-written by his friend, actress and comedy writer Arleen Sorkin and her partner Paul Slansky. Within a few months, 20th Century Fox had bought her the property and hired *Moonlighting* ace Glenn Gordon Caron to direct.

And yet despite her big screen success, everyone who has observed her on the set of *Friends* agrees that it is the place where she is happiest, where she feels most at home. "I just love it here," she said at the beginning of the new season. "This is something better than work."

The List

Director: **Mary Kay Place**
Writers: **Marta Kauffman & David Crane**

> *Ross and Rachel finally get together, only to have things fall apart when Rachel discovers Ross's rundown of her virtues and vices.*

version, and their response, is a bit more concise. "So I kissed her," he tells them as he chews his pizza. "Tongue?" asks Joey. Affirmative nods Ross. "Cool," Joey says.

But reality rears its ugly head the following day and Ross is guilt-ridden about what to do about his official girlfriend, Julie. His worst nightmare comes true as Julie unexpectedly walks in the door of Central Perk and both she and Rachel are standing there staring at him. Panicky, he tells Phoebe to play that song. "What song?" Phoebe asks. "You know...that song." So, Phoebe launches into an improvised ballad that just about says it all.

Real life is proving to be a major pain for Monica too. In fact, things have gotten so desperate on the job front that her only prospect is with a company that manufactures a synthetic chocolate

"Okay, why don't you two keep talking? I'll just ask the *toaster* for advice."

– Ross

IT HAS FINALLY HAPPENED. ROSS HAS KISSED RACHEL. And the girls go wild. They want to hear it all, every last detail. Everything! Rachel describes the monumental moment in pulp romance prose that has Monica and Phoebe swooning in adolescent ecstasy.

Across the hall, Ross, too, is bringing the guys up to speed on the night's events – although his

THE TWO OF THEM KISSED LAST NIGHT

There was a girl, we'll call her Betty,
There was a guy, let's call him Neal.
I can't stress this point too strongly.
None of these people are real.
But now our Neal must decide
Who will be the girl he casts aside.
Will Betty be the one that he loves truly
Or will it be the one we call...Loolie?
He must decide! He must decide!
Even though I made him up, he must
   decide.

Music by Lisa Kudrow.
Lyrics by Marta Kauffman and David Crane.

Rachel demands to see what's on the paper.

substitute called "Mock-late". The ingratiating Mr. Rastatter (guest star Michael McKean) tells her he's looking for chefs to create "Mock-late" holiday recipes and asks if she would be interested. Monica tries to say yes, but her mouthful of "Mock-late" seems to have hardened. Monica gets busy whipping up "Mock-late" taste treats but all her hard work falls flat when "Mock-late" is nixed by the FDA. Wait, it gets worse. She gets a call from Mr. Rastatter who wants to know if she ate any "Mock-late" while working on her recipes. And if so, by any chance, has she noticed a burning sensation when she pees?

Ross continues to agonize over what he should do about Julie, but Chandler has no sympathy for him and his two-girlfriend dilemma. Joey, on the other hand, thinks it's easily solvable: "I've got two words for you," he tells Ross, "threesome!" Chandler suggests that Ross make a list of the two girls' pros and cons. If nothing else, it'll give him something else to do on his new souped-up computer besides playing "Dune". Ross goes along reluctantly and starts off

by admitting that Rachel is a little spoiled. And a little ditzy. Oh, and a little too into her looks. And then there's the fact that Julie is a paleontologist like he is, while Rachel is just a waitress. "And," Joey chimes in, "her ankles are a little chubby." No doubt about it, Ross admits, Julie is wonderful. But she's got one fatal flaw. She's just not Rachel. Ross knows now what he's got to do. He's got to tell Julie the truth. So he does and it's awful. She cries. He cries. She throws things at him. They hit him. Whatever. It's over.

The next day at Chandler and Joey's, Rachel happens to see the Pro and Con list on Chandler's computer screen. Chandler slams the tell-tale machine shut, but suddenly the printer fires up. Rachel knows there's something about her on that paper. She grabs it and, well, you can just imagine. Ditzy! Spoiled! Just a waitress! Of course, the one that really gets her is the thing about the chubby ankles.

Was it only a few days ago that Ross was in a tizzy over having two girlfriends? Well, that's no longer a problem, because now he has none.

"The first time the cast read ["The One With The List"] at the table was the day that the O.J. verdict was announced. Afterwards, we had a notes session and one of the network people turned to me and David and said, like they usually do, 'So, where are you guys with [the script?]' whereupon I suddenly found myself saying, 'I don't know. I just don't care anymore. I don't care about Ross and Rachel and their stupid problems.' And then I began to sob hysterically. Then someone — I think it was Kevin — leaned over to the poor network person and said, 'I don't think this is about the script.'"

MARTA KAUFFMAN

Phoebe's Dad

Director:
Kevin S. Bright

Writers:
**Jeffrey Astrof
& Mike Sikowitz**

Ross manages to make things worse between him and Rachel, and Phoebe finds out that her father isn't really the guy whose picture comes in those fancy gift frames, but rather a pharmacist who lives in upstate New York.

**"Uh, Pheebs?
That's the guy
that comes in
the frame."**

– Chandler

IT'S CHRISTMAS TIME AND THE SPIRIT OF GOOD WILL is everywhere – except between Ross and Rachel who is still furious about the whole list thing. He says okay, he can respect that, so why doesn't she make a list about him? Oh, she says brightening, you mean like how you're whiney and wishy-washy and never ever ever seize the day and wear too much gel in your hair? That's what he means. She tells him he's absolutely right. She does feel better.

Ross slinks off to sit with the rest of the gang, dragging his shopping bags filled with holiday gifts. One of them, a picture frame, catches Phoebe's eye and she exclaims that it has a picture of her father in it. No really, she says, that's him. "I thought your father was in jail," someone says. "No," she says, "that's my stepfather. This is my real father who ran out on my mom and me before I was born." She can prove it, she says, and pulls out her wallet to show

them another generic photo that looks just like the one in the frame. Phoebe, honey, Monica says gently, that guy in the photo is a model. Phoebe doesn't know what to do with this concept.

Later that night, Phoebe's grandmother (guest star Audra Lindley) finally comes clean. "It was your mother's idea," she says. "I didn't want to go along with it, but then she died and it was harder to say no." Phoebe is devastated. "So he's not a famous tree surgeon in Burma?" she asks sadly. "Last I heard," her grandmother answers diffidently, "he was a pharmacist in upstate New York."

Down in the Village, Monica and Rachel are putting the finishing touches to their Christmas Eve party when they realize that it's gotten stiflingly hot. Ross, who has been busy driving them both nuts, tries to turn off the radiator but ends up breaking off the cap. The super says he can't replace it until after the holidays. Figures. Monica and Rachel tipped all the service guys in the building with Christmas cookies. Looks like it's tit-for-tat time.

Meanwhile, Phoebe spends hours calling every strange-sounding town in upstate New York for her father's number. Her grandmother thinks she's better off without the creep, but if she's that determined, she'll tell her where he is. She even loans

"Hey, look what I got for you. It's a Slinky! Remember? 'What walks down stairs, alone or in pairs, everyone knows it's ...' just a big spring."

— Ross —

her the cab. Chandler and Joey go along to give her moral support and to do some last minute shopping at the outlets on the way back.

It's already dark when Phoebe pulls up in front of a pretty frame house covered with Christmas decorations. But hours later she's only made it to the mailbox. She returns to the cab – where Joey and Chandler have fallen asleep. They wake up and ask her what happened. She can't do it, she tells them. She's already lost a fake dad, and she's just not ready to lose a real one.

Back at the party, it's about 104 degrees and the guests are turning into jerky. Ross decides to prove to Rachel that he's capable of seizing. He approaches the building super and slips him one hundred bucks to fix the radiator. The super pockets the bills and says thanks a lot, but he still can't get the part till after the holidays. "Good seizing, Gel Boy," Rachel jeers.

Much much later that night, Phoebe and company stumble in to find that they've missed the party. Chandler and Joey give out their presents – which they've gotten from the gas station on the turnpike. Toilet seat covers for Phoebe. Windshield wiper blades for Rachel. A can of soda for Ross. And a ribbed condom for Monica.

Ross says they shouldn't have. He really means it.

Russ

Director: **Thomas Schlamme**
Writer: **Ira Ungerleider**

Joey gets a job on Days of Our Lives *the old-fashioned way; Rachel is attracted to a guy who could be Ross's double; and Monica discovers that Fun Bobby isn't so much fun when he's not drinking.*

JOEY HAS GOTTEN MASSA-CRED IN THE REVIEWS OF his latest play and he's beginning to think it's time to pack it in. But then out of the blue, he gets a callback for *Days of Our Lives.* This is the break he's been wanting for ten years! But he's getting the feeling, he tells Chandler later, that he's going to have to sleep with the casting lady to get the part. Chandler asks him what she looks like. Joey says that she looks so good that if he'd met her in a bar, he'd be buying her breakfast. So what's the problem, Chandler asks. Still, Joey says, if he

"Wait a minute, wait a minute. I think this will change your mind: 'In a mediocre play, Joseph Tribbiani was able to achieve brilliant new levels of ... sucking.'"

– Monica –

ever really made it, he'd always wonder if it were because of his talent or the Little General.

"I didn't know we were seeing other people," Ross says to Rachel after he finds out she has a date with someone else. "We're not seeing each other," she points out. Okay, well if that's the way it is, he tells her, then maybe he'll go out with the woman from the moth department at the museum who's been buzzing him of late. But Ross isn't fooling anybody; he's crushed, as usual, and the gang feels terrible for him. Look, Rachel tells them after he leaves, they're just going to have to get used to the idea that she and Ross are not going to be together. Moreover, she's starting to get serious about this new guy Russ (guest star "Snarro" aka David Schwimmer) – who happens to walk in shortly after Ross leaves. There's a funny thing about Russ though, except for his longish hair and Jay Leno-esque chin, he's an absolute dead ringer for Ross. The others – espe-cially Phoebe – are spooked by the resemblance, but Rachel doesn't see it.

Monica is happy because Fun Bobby is back in her life. And she's not alone. Everybody is crazy about Fun Bobby. Even the guys. But then late one night after Bobby leaves, Rachel notices that they've gone through five bottles of wine – or rather that Fun Bobby has. Now that she's mentioned it, they all realize that Bobby always has a drink in his hand. Could Fun Bobby be a drunk? Monica confronts him and he agrees to cool it for her. The problem is that once he does, he becomes as dull as dirt. His sober idea of a funny story is telling her about how the light in his refrigerator burned out. Now she's so bored when they go out, she's taken up drinking herself.

Russ has become a regular at Central Perk, even though he often clashes with Ross – maybe because they're so much alike. For one thing, they're both doctors – although as Russ points out, he's a *real* one. Oh please, Ross says, you're a doctor of *gums*. They're also both weenies, as Chandler mutters. More prob-lematic, though, they're both in love with the same woman. As they bicker back and forth in the same maddeningly phlegmatic way, Rachel suddenly sees what Phoebe has been saying. They really *are* the same person. That does it for Russ.

Joey screws up his courage and goes in for the callback on *Days of Our Lives* and just as he feared, the cast-ing lady is all over him. But when he resists her advances, she offers him an even bigger part. "You are now looking at Dr. Drake Ramoray," he tells Chandler proudly when he gets home, "reoccur-ing in at least four episodes." And now he's gotta go take a shower.

How's this for irony? Fun Bobby breaks up with Monica because she has a drinking problem and he can't afford to be in a co-dependent situation. And even though Rachel has dumped the hapless Russ, he still stops by Central Perk. One day when he's there, Ross's old girlfriend Julie comes in. Her eyes meet Russ's and you can almost see Cupid's arrow ripping through their hearts. It must be love because the romantic music is so loud even Chandler and Phoebe can hear it.

For BB   Urgent ☐
Date _____ Time _____

While You Were Out

M _re: Julia Roberts_
Of _____
Phone _____
AREA CODE   NUMBER   EXTENSION

Telephoned ☐   Please Call ☐
Came To See You ☐   Will Call Again ☐
Returned Your Call ☐ Wants To See You ☐

Message _PTEase send_
video cassettes of first
season on "friends"
(she's a fan)
Signed _____

9711   ☐ ADAMS BUSINESS FORMS

Joey tells Chandler that if he got a job on *Days of Our Lives* after he slept with the casting lady, he would always wonder whether it was because of his talent or the "Little General."

John Shaffner, Art Director & Greg Grande, Set Designer

Monica's Apartment

THE BACK-STORY OF THE OLD BUILDING WHERE Joey, Chandler, Rachel and Monica live is that it's the six-storey apartment building on West 14th Street I lived in when I was in New York. My partner and I used it as a model because when we first read the script of *Friends*, we recognized ourselves in the characters, so we started to pull a lot of design information out of our memories – as opposed to books.

In doing the original design, we decided that Monica's place was a larger apartment that had been chopped in half – which they did all the time in New York in the '60s. We also thought that someone had torn down the wall between the kitchen and the living room. Kevin wanted a more film-like quality to the set. He wanted to be more in the set rather than on the outside looking in. So we took the top off of a rectangular room. We played with this business of rotating the room on its axis a little bit. Then – instead of having a hallway in the bedroom – which is a common way to design a sitcom, I thought it would be fun if the two bedroom doors opened up into the living room because then the movement could flow like that in a Feydeau farce. We also designed a hallway with the stairway in it and it occurred to me that we could put Joey and Chandler across the hall. Because of my experience in theater, I wanted to give the writers something to play with. Ultimately though, the real challenge in set design is seeing how far you can theatricalize reality … and yet still get the audience to follow you.

John Shaffner – Art Director

We did a basic model design for the pilot and then we went to lunch with Jim Burrows, the director of the pilot. He looked at the model and said we needed a single identifying feature about this apartment. He suggested a skylight. But we decided to try something more like a studio window. The window also gave us the opportunity to expand out to the back with a ledge that the characters could convert into a kind of terrace that you would have to crawl out of a window to get to.

After the first season, everyone asked us, "Where is that window?" So I went to New York and took pictures of a window just like it, so we could prove that it really did exist. Of course, they're not wildly common, but they are there. The thing about New York is whatever you imagine, you can find it there somewhere. It is that kind of city.

J.S.

The frame around the peephole in Monica's apartment was really a mistake. It originally had a mirror in it and one of the guys on the crew broke it. So, as I was detailing the apartment, I sort of hung it there till I could get back to it, but then when I looked at it, I thought it was kind of interesting and decided to leave it there. It became the most asked about design detail on the show.

Greg Grande – Set Designer

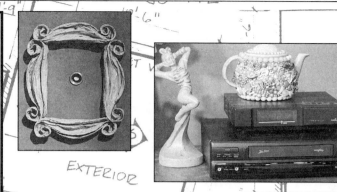

EXTERIOR

All the little objects in Monica's apartment she has either found at the flea market or on the street. Her work has never been steady, so she's never had much money to spend on her place, but obviously she's got a good eye. The one thing in Monica's apartment that's expensive is her stove. That's what she saved all her money for. Everything else is a found object or a hand-me-down.

J.S.

We were criticized a lot the first season because some people thought that you couldn't get an apartment that size in New York. But the idea is that it was Monica's grandmother's and that she got a sublease on it and then her grandmother died.

J.S.

Monica's cooking gave her a reason to be the mother to the group. That's why everyone comes over to her place – because she's the one who's got the food. And then of course she had been heavy as a youngster and now she's thin and has this love-hate relationship with food. That's why we gave her such an elaborate kitchen. However, if we'd known that Monica was such a neat-freak, I don't know if Greg and I would have gone quite so eclectic with the furnishings.

J.S.

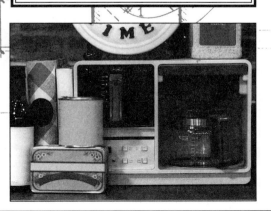

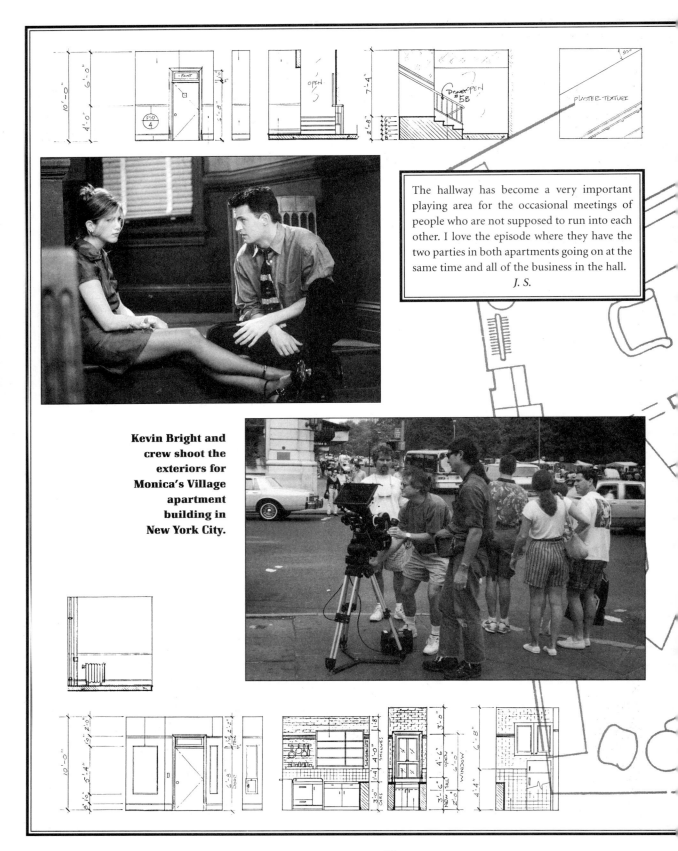

The hallway has become a very important playing area for the occasional meetings of people who are not supposed to run into each other. I love the episode where they have the two parties in both apartments going on at the same time and all of the business in the hall.
J. S.

Kevin Bright and crew shoot the exteriors for Monica's Village apartment building in New York City.

Central Perk

The coffeehouse was the final set to be built for the pilot. We wanted a place that had a lot of charm and warmth. Of course, we were old enough to remember the prototypical coffeehouses from the '60s. And then Kevin shot several small places in New York and brought us the photos.

Originally, the windows were frosted from about halfway down, so when people were in the restaurant you could only see a little bit through the top. When we moved to a bigger stage for our second season, I decided we should look out at our own little street. So we found three old storefronts here at Warner Bros. and we patched them together and created our own little piece of the Village.

J. S.

For Central Perk, I exaggerated the living room coffeehouse look that was – and still is – popular in L.A. and New York into a theater-like atmosphere with huge oversized Victorian furniture. I change the art in Central Perk for every show, just the way a village coffeehouse might display neighborhood artists. Some of it is by people on the crew.

G. G.

The Lesbian Wedding

Director: **Thomas Schlamme**
Writer: **Doty Abrams**

> *Phoebe is possessed by the spirit of a deceased octogenarian named Rose Edelman, and Ross forges an unlikely bond with his ex-wife and her lesbian lover that helps them all get through their (that's right) wedding ceremony.*

Carol and Susan's wedding ceremony is interrupted by an outburst from Rose Edelman, whose spirit has taken possession of Phoebe's body (with very special guest star, Candace Gingrich as the officiating minister).

CAROL AND SUSAN HAVE SOME EXCITING NEWS FOR Ross: they're getting married. "You mean as in 'I now pronounce you wife and wife' married?" he asks incredulously. They know it's got to be a little weird for him, but they want him to come.

Ross tries to play it cool, but the truth is he has no intention of going to the wedding. Even when it turns out that Monica is going to cater the affair. Monica can't believe it; you mean you're still not over Carol. "She's my ex-wife. If she were marrying a guy, you wouldn't expect me to be there," he says.

Joey is now playing Dr. Drake Ramoray on *Days of Our Lives*! And he's actually pretty good. Well, he does have a secret, he confides to the gang. It's the "smell-the-fart" school of soap opera acting where you stare intently into space while you try to remember your line.

Phoebe's life isn't exactly uneventful either. An 82-year-old client of hers named Rose Edelman dies while she's massaging her aura and her spirit passes into Phoebe's body. So now at the most unexpected moments, Phoebe lapses into Rose's voice and says things like "I know who it is you remind me of ... Evelyn Dermer. Of course, that was before she got the lousy facelift. Now she looks like Soupy Sales." Phoebe feels that Rose has unfinished business on earth, so she asks Rose's husband for some insight. Mr. Edelman turns out to be some kind of cutie (beloved character actor, Phil Leeds) and a rascal to boot. "Rose wanted to see everything," he assures Phoebe. "Everything?" Phoebe asks. "Everything," he declares. "Oh, and she also wanted to sleep with me one last time."

Rachel's mother (guest star, Marlo Thomas) stops by to see how Rachel's doing in her new life. Rachel is a nervous wreck fearing she'll think "because she didn't marry Barry, her life is total crap." But her mother thinks she's got a great life...so great, in fact, she wants it for herself. Yes, she's come to tell Rachel that she and her father are getting a divorce. Rachel goes into total shock. "I married my Barry," her mother explains, "you didn't." She wants a second chance at life, at freedom, and at fun. Speaking of which, she wants Rachel and Monica to clue her in to what's new in sex and, oh, does anybody have any marijuana?

Rachel is stunned by this news and especially by the strange person claiming to be her mother. The always-supportive Chandler tells Rachel to look on the bright side. "When my parents got divorced, they sent me to a shrink who said all children have a tendency to blame themselves, but in your case it's actually true."

Meanwhile, Phoebe is taking Rose everywhere – Rockefeller Center, the Statue of Liberty. The only problem is she needs to go to the bathroom a lot.

Back home, Monica has under-estimated her prep time for the wedding food. The gang – minus Ross – pitches in to help, but she still panics as only she can. "All right people, we're in trouble here. We've only got 12 hours and 36 minutes left. Move! Move! Move!" Chandler suggests that she should have German subtitles. Finally she invokes the ultimate threat: she threatens to cry.

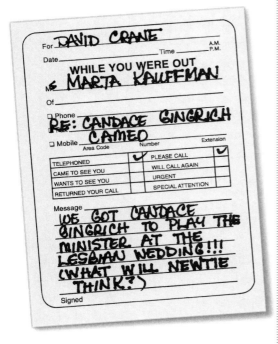

For DAVID CRANE   A.M. / P.M.
Date _____ Time _____
WHILE YOU WERE OUT
M₅ MARTA KAUFFMAN
Of _____
☐ Phone
RE: CANDACE GINGRICH CAMEO
☐ Mobile Area Code ___ Number ___ Extension ___

TELEPHONED	✓	PLEASE CALL	✓
CAME TO SEE YOU		WILL CALL AGAIN	
WANTS TO SEE YOU		URGENT	
RETURNED YOUR CALL		SPECIAL ATTENTION	

Message WE GOT CANDACE GINGRICH TO PLAY THE MINISTER AT THE LESBIAN WEDDING!!! (WHAT WILL NEWTIE THINK?)
Signed _____

In the midst of the catering chaos, a distraught Carol shows up and announces that the wedding is off. Her parents were supposed to give her away, but now they're boycotting the ceremony. Then she and Susan had a fight when Susan said the wedding wasn't about parents or anything else but their love. Ross can't believe it, but he actually thinks Susan's right and tells Carol so. In fact, he talks her into patching things up with her.

Ross ends up escorting Carol down the aisle. It goes well even though he has a little problem letting go of her when the time comes. The food is a big hit so Monica is happy. Rachel's mother is happy because three of the guests made eyes at her. Susan is so happy that she asks Ross to dance and offers to let him lead. Even Mrs. Edelman enjoys herself although at first she was somewhat taken aback and croaked, "Oh, my God! Now I've seen everything!" in the middle of the ceremony. The only grumblers are Chandler and Joey who find it plenty frustrating

"It just seems so futile. All these women and … nothing. It's like I'm Superman without my powers. I have the cape, and yet I cannot fly."
– *Joey*

to be surrounded by a roomful of unavailable women. Joey complains, "I feel like Superman without powers." To which Chandler replies, "Now you know how I feel every single day. The world is my lesbian wedding."

"David and I had met Candace Gingrich at the GLADD awards and we got to thinking that it would be a really nice bit of casting to use her as the minister at Carol and Susan's wedding. Not only was she wonderful in the role, she did a beautiful piece of writing for it. Alexa Junge originally had the minister saying, 'there's nothing that pleases me more than when two people come together in love' and Candace asked if she could change it to 'there's nothing that pleases God more than when two people come together in love.' It was such a wonderful moment. I still get chills when I think about it."

MARTA KAUFFMAN

David Crane, Marta Kauffman and Kevin Bright take a break on the set of "The One With The Lesbian Wedding" with That Girl Marlo Thomas and That Lesbian Sister of Speaker of the House, Candace Gingrich.

PHOEBE

I don't know how to say this,
but... I have this suspicion that
when your wife's spirit left her
body, it kind of... stuck around.

MR. ADELMAN

That is so like her. She could
never leave a place. She has to
get a recipe, she has to find her
glasses... I've probably spent a
good six years of my life waiting
with the car.

I LOVE THIS BUT IT'S *
TOO LONG *
CUT?
M.K.

PHOEBE

Actually, I think she stuck
around... in me.

MR. ADELMAN

You're saying my wife is in you?

← *WE GOT PHIL LEEDS* *
(who's that?)
A GREAT OLD CHARACTER GUY YOU'LL KNOW HIM WHEN YOU SEE HIM.

PHOEBE

Look, you don't have to believe
me. Just tell me this: did she
have any unfinished business? Can
you think of any reason why she'd
be hanging around?

"Carol and Susan are based on our two best friends in New York. We didn't create them for any particular political reason or because of lesbian chic. It was just an opportunity to tell a really interesting story. Or anyway, that's what we thought until the beginning of the season when the show was moved to 8 o'clock and our friends called us to say that their little daughter had seen Carol and Susan and looked up at them with big eyes and said 'Look Mommy, a family like ours on TV.' That was when we first understood why we had done it."

MARTA KAUFFMAN AND DAVID CRANE

The Superbowl Parts I & II

There are stars galore in this episode as Monica and Rachel tangle over Jean-Claude Van Damme; Phoebe gets a gig from an admiring fan (Chris Isaak); Chandler is reunited with Susie Underpants (Julia Roberts) from his fourth grade class; Joey faces off with a beautiful stalker (Brooke Shields) and Ross is reunited with Marcel (the monkey).

Director parts I & II:
Michael Lembeck
Writers part I:
**Jeffrey Astrof
& Mike Sikowitz**
Writer part II:
Michael Borkow

"Hitting her with a frying pan is a good idea, but let's have a backup plan in case she isn't a cartoon character!"
– Chandler

FAME HAS COME AT LAST TO JOEY TRIBBIANI – whose role as Dr. Drake Ramoray on *Days of Our Lives* has earned him his very own stalker. First she leaves a note, then she shows up out of the blue, scaring Joey and Chandler to death. But when Joey throws open the door, he discovers that his stalker, Erika (guest star Brooke Shields) is a stone knock-out. So, she's a total wack job, you see him thinking, but hey, everybody's gotta go some time.

At lunch with her the next day, Erika – who has a little problem in distinguishing between TV and real life – tells Joey that she can't believe it was only an hour ago that he was reattaching Sabrina's spinal cord. Enraptured by his "miracle, life-giving hands," she asks if she can lick them. She loves his fingers so much she could bite them off, she tells him. Joey says that would be a problem because his watch would fall off. She laughs loudly at his little joke. Very loudly. But then, someone starts to choke in the restaurant and yet Dr. Drake Ramoray doesn't come to the rescue. Joey explains that he is, uh, a neurosurgeon and that was clearly a case of "foodal chokage."

When Erika comes storming into Joey and Chandler's one night in a fit of jealous rage, he tries again to convince her that he's only an actor. But

Joey's stalker (guest star Brooke Shields) loves his fingers so much she could bite them off.

PHOEBE'S GRANDMA SONG.

Now grandma's a person that
    everyone likes,
She brought you a train and a big
    shiny bike.
But lately she hasn't been coming
    to dinner.
And last time you saw her she looked
    so much thinner.
Your mom and your dad said she
    moved to Peru,
But the truth is she died and some day
    you will too.
La-la-la-la-la-la-la

Music by Lisa Kudrow.
Lyrics by Jeff Astrof and Mike Sikowitz.

Producer Kevin Bright, Lisa Kudrow and Chris Isaak fool around during a break on "The One After The Superbowl".

she still doesn't get it. Ross comes to the rescue by telling her that he's really Hans Ramoray, Drake's evil twin. The others back him up and then each one throws water in Hans's evil face. Erika sets out to find the real Dr. Drake.

Phoebe has a fan too – a really cute guy (guest star Chris Isaak) who wants her to sing for a children's group at the library. She agrees to do it, even though she's nervous because kids, unlike adults, actually listen. She tells him she'll just picture them in their underwear. But he thinks she shouldn't since that's what got the last guy fired. He kisses her and she's suddenly better. The kids like her too.

Afterwards he tells her that the kids loved her because she told the truth, and no one ever does that with kids. There is just one thing, though, the parents would be a little more comfortable if she would sing songs about barnyard animals. They're in luck because she just happens to have such a song. It's about how the cow in the meadow goes moo, and "the farmer hits him on the head and that's how we get hamburger." This goes over about as well as the dead grandmother in the previous song and Phoebe is fired. But Rob was right, the kids do love her. They track her down at Central Perk and clamor to hear her sing the songs that tell the truth.

Meanwhile, things are stalled between Ross and Rachel and he's so lonely that he's been missing Marcel, the monkey. He really loved that little guy – even if he did leave little monkey raisins in his hat and hump everything in sight. He decides to visit

(Left) **Susie wants Chandler to wear her hot pink thong to the restaurant.** (Below) **Susie tells Chandler to meet her in the men's room in "The One After The Superbowl".**

Marcel at the zoo. But when he gets there, an unctuous zoo official (guest star Fred Willard) informs him that Marcel has passed on. But as Ross turns to walk away, a weasely-looking cleanup guy sidles up to him and hisses, "Your monkey's *alive*!" The truth is that there was a break-in and Marcel was stolen. Word on the street is that he's got a new career in show business.

Indeed, Marcel has landed smartly on his little paws. He's making an action adventure movie on location in New York City. Ross and the rest of the gang set out to surprise him on the set. So, just how big a star is Marcel, they ask one of the crew guys. About like Cybil Sheppard, the guy answers. They are definitely impressed.

While lurking around the set, Chandler runs into Susie (guest star Julia Roberts), who was in his fourth grade class. She reminds him that he pulled up her skirt during a school play and the entire auditorium saw her underpants, but he doesn't really remember. Not one to hold a grudge, she asks him out.

Susie proves to be the woman of Chandler's dreams. She's beautiful. She's sweet. And most importantly, the woman is a freak. She wants to do it in elevators. (Or anyway, she *says* she does.) She even wants him to wear her panties when they go out to dinner. What more can a man ask? Once in the restaurant, Susie tells him to meet her in the

men's room. He's out of there like a flash. They slip into a stall and she orders him to undress. "Oooh, somebody's been doing their Buns of Steel Video," she coos admiringly. But then she grabs his clothes and bolts for the door. "I was Susie Underpants until I was eighteen!" she yells. "How can you still be upset about *that*?" Chandler asks in amazement. "Call me in twenty years and tell me if you're still upset about this," she snorts as she bounds through the door.

Joey enters the men's room to find Chandler cringing in the stall. "Give me your underpants," Chandler hisses. But Joey isn't wearing any.

Chandler is outraged. "Oh sure, I'm getting heat for not wearing underpants from the guy in the hot pink thong." Chandler has no choice. It's either do something drastic or live in the men's room for the rest of his life. A few minutes later he strides through the restaurant, his mid-section covered only by the stall door.

The next day as Monica and Rachel stroll around the location shoot, they catch sight of Jean-Claude Van Damme, the star of the movie. Monica inveigles Rachel to tell him she thinks he's cute. Unfortunately for her, Jean-Claude thinks Rachel is cute and he asks her out. The day after their date, Rachel is so insufferably smug and so not-at-all guilty that Monica flicks her. This leads to a slapping-hitting girl fight and Phoebe is forced to intervene. She pinches their earlobes and holds them apart until they promise to behave themselves. "If we were in prison," she observes cheerfully, "you two would be my bitches."

(Top left) "Uh, Joey, some people don't like that." – *Ross*
(Left) "Wow, talk about bad luck. The first time you try on panties, and someone walks off with your clothes." – *Joey*
(Below left) "'The Muscles from Brussels'? 'Wham, Bam Van Damme'? Did you see *Timecop*? Oh my God! He, like, totally changed time!" – *Monica*

For MARTA

Date _____ Time _____ A.M. P.M.

WHILE YOU WERE OUT

M _____
Of _____
☐ Phone _____
☐ Fax _____
☐ Mobile _____
   Area Code   Number   Extension

TELEPHONED	PLEASE CALL
CAME TO SEE YOU	WILL CALL AGAIN
WANTS TO SEE YOU	URGENT
RETURNED YOUR CALL	SPECIAL ATTENTION

Message THE STUDIO HAS GIVEN A NOTE THAT BY USING "LOOKS LIKE WE MADE IT" UNDER THE ROSS/MARCEL MONTAGE IT MIGHT GIVE THE AUDIENCE THE IMPRESSION THAT ROSS AND THE MONKEY ARE LOVERS... YEAH RIGHT!

Signed K. BRIGHT

Monica gets a turn with Jean-Claude, but only after Rachel assures him that Monica would love to join him and Drew Barrymore in a threesome. Naturally, that means that Monica has to beat up Rachel again. This time, Monica molests Rachel's favorite sweater and Rachel pours marinara sauce into Monica's purse. Obviously they're both going to have to kiss off the Muscles from Brussels. And they do. With gusto. They stand firm even when he tries to lure them into a threesome by boasting that he can crush a walnut with his butt.

And finally, Ross and Marcel spend a romantic day together with a Barry Manilow song playing in the background. And Joey lands a part in Marcel's film playing a soldier dying from poison gas. But he's so hammy, they end up killing him off.

(Right) **Well, we know why He's smiling anyway ...**

"Don't attribute this to me, but like Jean-Claude Van Damme doesn't have a great comic delivery. His thing is obviously leaping around. So we had these funny lines, but they weren't funny on him. So we had to come up with lines that were Van Damme-proof. So I would say them in a really horrible French accent, putting the emphasis on the wrong word and if people still laughed, then we pitched them to Van Damme. And that's how we came up with his 'I can crack a walnut with my butt.'"

ADAM CHASE

(Below) **Joey tries to steal the scene from Jean-Claude Van Damme.**

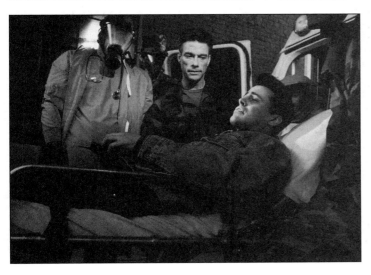

Bright Kauffman Crane *productions*

TO: Michael Lembeck

The women are complaining that J.C.V is sticking his tongue down their throats during the kiss-off scene. Can you do something with him?

Thanks

K.B

The Prom Video

Director:
James Burrows

Writer:
Alexa Junge

Joey gives Chandler a tacky token of his affection that seems destined to ruin his life; Monica asks her parents for a loan; and an old home video briefly brings Ross and Rachel back together.

JOEY HAS STARTED TO MAKE some money on *Days of Our Lives* and he's finally able to pay Chandler back for all the pizza and loans he's staked him to over the last year. And as a special surprise, he's also gotten him a very expensive, very Italian Stallion gold ID bracelet engraved with the words "To My Best Bud". The bracelet is so not Chandler. But what can he do?

"Wow. Is this friendship? I think so. Check it out. Bracelet buddies."

– Joey –

Monica, on the other hand, is so broke she may not be able to make this month's rent. Ross offers to give her a loan, but she says it would make her feel too guilty and tense every time she saw him. He says, in that case she should borrow it from their parents, since she feels that way about them anyway. And she does, when they come in to town to bring her some odds and ends from her old room the next day. But all her father comes up with is a twenty-dollar bill. Looks like Ross will be footing the rent after all.

But that's the least of his problems. Rachel is dating and it's killing him. Phoebe tells him to hang in there, that Rachel is his lobster. "It's a known fact that lobsters mate for life," Phoebe explains. "You can even see old lobster couples walking around their tank holding claws."

Later, at Central Perk, when Ross sees Rachel flirting with a new guy, he convinces himself that he is annoying her and it's up to him to save her – which he does in a very goofy way. He tries to tell her that she's his lobster, but for some reason this doesn't make any sense to her.

Chandler wears Joey's bracelet – even though the mere sight of it on his wrist makes a totally hot babe who'd been making eyes at him suddenly grab her coat and bolt for the door. "He couldn't have gotten me a VCR," he rants to Phoebe, "he has to get

---

TRUE FACT.

"When Courteney first appeared on the set in her (heavier) make-up and costume, she walked by Matthew Perry and said 'Hey.' He did not recognize her."

---

me the woman repeller, the reject from the Mr. T Collection." It probably would've been good for him to vent, if Joey hadn't walked in about half way through the rant. Clearly hurt, Joey turns on his heel and makes for the door as fast as the babe.

At home later, Joey tells Chandler that if he hated the bracelet so much, he should have said so. Chandler says no, he loves it and promises that he'll never take it

---

REGARDING THE VIDEO PART.

"Originally the song pitched for Ross to play on the Casio key-board was 'The Sting' (my brother Ben used to play that on his Casio). It was Mike Sikowitz's brilliant idea to have Ross play the theme from *Beverly Hills Cop*."

---

off, but then he looks down at his wrist and … the bracelet's gone. After he buys a replacement, Rachel informs him that (of course) Gunther found the other one. Now he has two incredibly tacky gold bracelets. Then Joey walks in and asks him what the deal is. "So we can both have one," Chandler improvises. "Is this friendship?" Joey shouts happily, "I think so!"

Back at the apartment, Phoebe is looking through the box of Monica's old things. What's this, she asks, as she holds up a huge bathing suit that looks like it could be an old Roseanne reject. "Oh that's mine," Monica says, "I used to be bigger then." Chandler says he thought it was something they used to cover Connecticut. The box then yields yet another embarrassing vestige of the past, a home video shot on prom night showing a very pudgy Monica and Rachel with her old nose. Ross, sporting a huge walrus mustache, lurks in the background. He says hardly a word and yet it's clear that he was in love with Rachel all those years ago. He even tries to come to the rescue when it looks like Rachel's date is going to stand her up. But just as he's coming down the stairs in his father's tux, he sees Rachel and her date bouncing out the door. Everyone is touched – especially Rachel, who walks slowly over to Ross, takes his face in her hands and kisses him deeply.

"See…he *is* her lobster," Phoebe says.

"The last moment in the episode – when Rachel goes to Ross and kisses him (which James Burrows referred to as 'the longest cross in the history of television') was inspired by a moment from *Fiddler on the Roof* – when the student character crosses to Tevya's middle daughter and asks her to dance. Several writing staff members are Musical Theatre Nerds. The rest of the staff gives them much grief about this, but they don't have any right to talk since they have each seen *Star Wars* more times than Monica's prom date did (317)."

ALEXA JUNGE

Courteney Cox

"I thought she'd be a little aloof and celebrity-ish. But she wasn't at all."

Lisa Kudrow on Courteney Cox

SHE CAN TURN THE WORLD ON WITH HER SMILE. NO, she's not Mary Tyler Moore – although it's no wonder that informed pre-*Friends* speculation had it that Courteney Cox would inevitably prevail as the Mary Tyler Moore focal point of the then new situation comedy. Like Mary Richards, Cox's Monica

"Courteney has a tendency to be very frank ... sometimes shockingly so," says Tom Selleck of his provocative love interest on *Friends*, "but you always know where you stand with her."

Geller plays den mother to a band of lovable neurotics. And like Mary Tyler Moore at the start of her eponymous sitcom, Cox was the lone Name in the cast – the one with both a hit movie (*Ace Ventura: Pet Detective*) and a hit TV show (*Family Ties*) under her belt. And more importantly, she was the girl who had danced with the Boss (Bruce Springsteen).

David Schwimmer now acknowledges that Cox made everyone else in the cast a little nervous when they first got together to rehearse. But being a smart little thing, Cece (as her friends call her) set out to kill off that potentially disruptive vibe with a pre-emptive strike. "She was actually the first person to speak up about us being a team," Matthew Perry says. "It was our second day at work, and we went outside on a break together and she said, 'This is an ensemble show. I think we should really all try to help each other out.' Everybody just jumped on that." Cox went on to postulate pointedly that there was no Seinfeld in the group. "We're all a team, so if you guys have a suggestion for me, or if I have one for you guys, I'd love to say it, and I hope you'll be able to say it, too." Cox understood the difference because she herself had been the odd man out in a show where the star pecking order was firmly entrenched, having made her entrance to *Family Ties* five years into its seven-year run.

So much for Cox's status within the cast. The next question is … is she or isn't she … a neat freak … a compulsive … a neurotic mass of insecurities like Monica Geller? After a great deal of research into the matter, it's safe to say…yes and no. And here's why; Cox herself has actually been quoted as saying, "I *am* Monica Geller." Of course, that utterance came at the outset of the show's sudden popularity explosion when everyone involved was a little giddy. Little did Courteney Cox know that so many millions would decide – as TV viewers will – to take her throwaway line literally. The truth is far more complicated than that. But, happily, only in the nicest way.

From all accounts of those who know her best – and you'll be interested to know that this group does not include Pamela Anderson or any of the Brat Pack – Cece shares with Monica a high level of energy, and a sense of duty and discipline. According to them, she's one of those people who somehow manages to be in two places at once. She's as busy as a corporate CEO and yet she always makes time for friends in need. When not playing mother hen to the cast, she's always on the move. "I need to see change constantly," she says, "and when I feel like I've taken it to the limits, then I need to move on. I think it's just part of my personality. I get bored easily." However, she insists, "I'm not a neat freak. And I'm not obsessed. [And] The anorexia stuff is bullshit." On the other hand, Cox lobbied hard for the part of Monica even though the producers wanted her for Rachel, the pampered Long Island princess. "They thought I seemed too vulnerable to play Monica. And I went, 'then you don't know me at all.'" Let's just say that Cox is Monica minus the neuroses and the money troubles and certainly minus the boyfriend woes – an aspect of her character's life that has been somewhat difficult for professional quibblers to swallow. Cox is an uprooted Steel Magnolia who is disciplined and focused and who uses her natural gifts intelligently. And if you don't believe it, consider her astonishing rise to fame.

Courteney Cox was born on 15 June 1964 in the country club suburbs of Birmingham, Alabama, the

Costume design by
Debra McGuire

— 51 —

CasACTRESS

COURTENEY COX

****THEATRICAL FILM		1993
		1991
ACE VENTURA	MIRAMAX	1991
		1990
RULES OF THE GAME	NEO PICTURES	1990
SHAKING THE TREE	WALT DISNEY	1988
BLUE DESERT	TWENTIETH CENTURY FOX	1987
MR. DESTINY	CANNON PICTURES, INC.	1986
COCOON II	CANNON PICTURES, INC.	
MASTER OF THE UNIVERSE		
DOWN TWISTED		

***FILM T.V.		1994
	CASTLEROCK	1993
	LORIMAR	1992
SEINFELD		1991
TROUBLE WITH LARRY	ROB REINER PROD	1990
TOPPER	UNIVERSAL TELEVISION	1989
MORTON AND HAYS	QUINTEX ENTERT	1989
CURIOSITY KILLS	STEVE KRANTZ PRODS.	1988
PRIZE PULITZER	NBC PRODUCTIONS	1987
TILL WE MEET AGAIN	MGM/ PATH	
A ROCKPORT CHRISTMAS		
IF IT'S TUESDAY, IT STILL MUST BE BELGIM		

***TAPE T.V.		1987
	PARAMOUNT	1986
	NBC PRODUCTIONS	1985
	UNIVERSAL TELEVISION	
		1985

She was the one with the hit movie and TV show

youngest of four children (two sisters, Virginia and Dottie, and one brother, Richard). Her parents divorced when she was ten years old. Both parents remarried two years later and nine stepchildren were added to the mix. "I think because my parents did get divorced, I felt there were a lot of things I had to accomplish. I think I grew up fast, not always emotionally but I had to take care of myself." As a budding southern belle, she hooked up with all the right clubs, showed up at all the right cotillions and was instilled with all the proper genteel southern pretensions. Although there were mild episodes of rebelliousness, Cox stayed for the most part on the straight and narrow – graduating from high school and then enrolling in college where she intended to study to become an architect. But the summer before her freshman year, she took the advice of her step-father's brother, Miles Copeland, Sr., a former CIA operative who – based perhaps on her comeliness, or perhaps on her drive – strongly advised her to go to New York before grounding herself in a conventional southern life. To Cox's great advantage, Copeland Sr.'s sons would provide support and serious entrée for the callow Alabama girl. Miles Jr., president of IRS Records, Ian, the head of FBI, New York's trendiest rock'n'roll booking agency, and Stewart, the drummer for and co-founder of the Police, had become three of the music business's most powerful players.

At Ian Copeland's urging, Courteney set out to become a model and an actress. With the help of the Copeland clan, she landed a contract with the prestigious Ford modeling agency. She became one of those fresh-faced girls whose sunny countenances

> "If there's a hair on my food, I'm one of those people who will eat the food anyway."
>
> COURTENEY COX

appear on teen magazines like *Tiger Beat* and *Young Miss* as well as the covers of romance novels aimed at young women. After a summer in New York, she went to Washington, D.C., to attend her freshman year in college. She then returned to New York – where she filmed commercials for Noxema, Maybelline, and most notably Tampax, wherein she made TV history by uttering the then-forbidden word "period", referring to her menstrual cycle rather than the little dot that comes at the end of a sentence. She also landed a two-day walk-on part as a debutante named Bunny on the long-running New York soap opera, *As the World Turns*. All the while Cox was preparing herself for bigger things…taking speech lessons to lose her southern accent and acting lessons so as to negotiate the well-traveled path from model to actress. And then came the legendary Big Break for which she remains famous today. In 1984, Cox went to a casting "cattle call" for a brief cameo in a Bruce Springsteen video in which the script called for the Boss to pull a fan up on to the stage for a flirtatious *pas-de-deux*. "There were lots of dancers there…these great long-legged women, and I'm wearing jeans and sneakers, and I went 'whoa, I'm in the wrong place.'" But if the Boss had pulled one of those show biz types out of the audience, the scene wouldn't have played as the egalitarian gesture Springsteen's carefully crafted image as a Regular Joe demands. The video's director Brian de Palma wanted the little interlude to look like a piece of video *verité* and that meant choosing a girl who looked like the real thing. All told, Cox was in the video only 26 seconds, but her bashful Every Girl created an indelible image that endures to this day. She says now that the part didn't change her fortunes all that radically, but it did open a lot of doors. And it no doubt gave her extra Cool Points with the very hip producers of *Friends*.

In 1985, Cox signed on to *Misfits of Science* – her first TV series. But neither the show, nor her first two feature-film outings – *Down Twisted* and *Masters of the Universe* – did her any justice. It was her role as Lauren, Michael J. Fox's girlfriend, on *Family Ties* that once again brought her to the attention of the great American unwashed. After that show closed up shop, she did a couple of film appearances in several non-memorable films like *Cocoon: the Return* and *Mr. Destiny*. But, as everyone who hasn't been stranded on the space station Mir knows, her next

film – the low-budget quickie, *Ace Ventura: Pet Detective* – ended up one of the all-time comedy blockbusters. Yet despite her presence in several world class comedies, the world had no idea that the lovely Courteney could be funny. It was not until her inspired turn as Monica Geller that we realized that this babe could not only get laughs, she could act. How else can you explain her ability to make us believe that she is someone who has the same trouble getting and keeping a lover as lesser mortals.

"Let's face it," she says on that much-dissed and discussed topic, "we've all got problems. We don't choose the right people, we've all got hang-ups. It's hard in life anyway to find the right person." And in fact, Cox herself is now "totally single" and insists that she doesn't get asked on that many dates "because you have to put yourself in situations where you get asked out." Pretty amazing, given her status as – as one magazine recently put it – a quasi-goddess. But Cox demurs on that score: "I don't have the highest esteem when it comes to that," she says. "I think that sometimes in certain photographs, given the right hair and make-up and the right lighting I can look okay, but I don't look at myself in a very healthy way."

'Atta girl, Monica…er, Courteney. That's why we love you. Don't ever change.

The good-natured Courteney Cox puts up with Matthew Perry's between-scene antics.

Ross And Rachel ... You Know

Director:
Michael Lembeck

Writers:
**Michael Curtis &
Gregory Malins**

After a traumatic first attempt, Ross and Rachel finally cross "that line"; Monica falls for a family friend who's twenty years older; and Chandler and Joey devolve into a species best described as "Lord of the Flies Meets Beavis and Butthead."

Joey and Chandler have their pizza delivered to Monica's so they won't have to move from their recliners to answer the door.

ROSS AND RACHEL GO OUT TO A MOVIE ON THEIR first official date as Not Just Friends. After making sure they're alone in the apartment, they slowly drift toward each other and embrace. But Rachel can't keep from laughing. She tells Ross she's just nervous, that they're crossing "that line" and it's a very big thing. They try again, but she still can't keep from giggling. Okay, she's got it together, she promises. But now Ross is self-conscious. She demands that he grab her ass, but he refuses. She tries backing up into his hands, but his romantic ardor has gone flat.

Joey's soap has picked up his option and he celebrates by buying a big screen TV and matching Lazy Boys for him and Chandler. They decide to stay in their chairs for the rest of their lives. They order pizza and Chinese food and have it delivered across the hall so they won't have to answer the door. They stop drinking soda so they won't have to get up to pee. Mostly monosyllabic, they bellow when anyone gets in the way of the screen. Phoebe is worried. "You've got to go outside with the three-dimensional people," she beseeches them. "No! Outside bad!" Joey grunts. "Inside good."

Monica is catering a party for Dr. Richard Burke (guest star Tom Selleck), an old friend of her parents. And Phoebe is helping her out. Dr. Burke hasn't seen Monica since she was a kid and he is clearly impressed with how she's grown up.

Dr. Burke has split up with his wife of thirty years, he tells the women, and he's trying to get back into the swing of things with this party. But his friends don't interest him nearly as much as the lovely Monica. Phoebe says he's smitten with her. Get real, Monica tells her: he's a grownup and almost twenty years older.

Ross and Rachel are headed out for their Big Date. What a coincidence, Monica says, she's going out too. Ross is stunned to hear that it's with their parents' friend Dr. Burke, but Monica warns him to mind his own business. Then he gets an emergency call from the museum telling him to get in as quickly as possible. Rachel goes along with him and sits alone in one of the dioramas while he rushes around. All dressed up with nothing to do, she entertains herself by peeking under one of the prehistoric men's loincloths.

Back at the apartment, Monica and Richard look at photos of his daughter and grandchild. "Are we nuts

"What? I think it's great that he's, like, fifty. I mean, he'll be an inspiration to men who are almost retired all over the world."

— Ross —

here?" he suddenly asks her. She knows what he means. "I'm dating a man whose pool I once peed in," she jokes weakly. He reluctantly gets up to leave. "This really sucks," Monica says. Richard agrees. "We don't have to decide anything right now, do we?" he asks hopefully as he takes her in his arms. Then a pizza delivery arrives for the boys.

"We'll just do it another night," Rachel says when Ross finally finishes. But he has other ideas; he takes her into the planetarium and starts the stars spinning in the fake heavens. They wake up the next morning lying in each other's arms in one of the exhibits. It would be an incredibly romantic moment if only a class of seven-year-olds weren't staring at them and giggling in disbelief.

> "Courteney is the cutest thing in the world. I just want to eat her up! I want her to come home with me and stay with me and be my best friend for the rest of my life!"
>
> MARTA KAUFFMAN

"`...Ross and Rachel... You Know" Final Draft (1/5/96)

HE PULLS OFF HER BLAZER. WHILE HE IS TAKING OFF HIS
OWN JACKET, SHE LOOSENS HIS TIE AND GOES TO PULL IT
OFF OVER HIS HEAD. HOWEVER, THE KNOT GETS CAUGHT ON
HIS NOSE. HIS HANDS ARE TANGLED BEHIND HIS BACK.

                    ROSS

          Loosen the knot! Loosen the knot!

SHE DOES AND THE TIE COMES OFF. THEY KISS AGAIN.

                    ROSS (CONT'D)

          I can't believe this is happening.

                    RACHEL

          I know.

PASSIONATE, THEY ROLL ON THE FLOOR. AFTER A MOMENT,
RACHEL STOPS, PULLED UP SHORT.

                    RACHEL (CONT'D)

          (DISAPPOINTED, BUT TENDER) Oh, no.

          Oh. Oh, honey. That's okay.

                    ROSS

          What? (GETTING IT) Oh, no. you

          just rolled onto the juice box.

                    RACHEL

          (DEEPLY RELIEVED) Oh. Thank god.

THEY GO BACK TO KISSING. AS THE PASSION MOUNTS, WE
PAN UP TO THE CEILING. HEAVENS ARE EXPLODING. STARS
COLLIDE. AND WE...

                                        DISSOLVE TO:

THE NETWORK DOESN'T YET REALIZE THIS IS A PREMATURE EJACULATION JOKE -- D.C.

Joey Moves Out

Phoebe persuades Rachel to have a tattoo, although she herself chickens out; Chandler is hurt when Joey moves to a fancy new pad; and Monica tells her parents that their old friend Richard is her new boyfriend.

Director:
Michael Lembeck
Writer:
Betsy Borns

PHOEBE HAS TALKED RACHEL INTO GETTING A tattoo, but Rachel doesn't want Ross to know because he's bound to disapprove. Rachel starts to get cold feet as they look at designs in the tattoo parlor. "Is your boyfriend the boss of you," Phoebe demands. "Well, then who is?" "You?" Rachel answers meekly. Phoebe tells her to march her little heiny in there and get that heart tattooed on her butt.

It's Jack's birthday, and there's going to be a party. This will be the first time Monica will be in the same place with both her parents and Richard. He suggests that

> **"Look, I don't know what you're getting so bent out of shape for. It's not like we were going to live together forever. I mean, we're not Bert and Ernie."**
>
> *– Joey –*

they just tell them and get it over with, but Monica thinks she'd rather not give her father a stroke.

Joey has a chance to rent a big fancy apartment from a guy he works with on his soap. He figures it's not a bad idea seeing as he and Chandler have been fighting a lot lately over his using Chandler's toothbrush and licking the spoons instead of washing them. Even so, Chandler's hurt when Joey tells him he's considering moving. "It's not like we were going to live together forever," Joey tells him. "We're not Bert and Ernie."

"You guys are gonna come visit me, aren't you?" Joey asks

"Now, you march your heiny in there and get that little heart tattooed on your hip! Go! Wow. I don't even have mine yet and it's already making me tougher."

– Phoebe –

everyone. "Sure, you got the big TV," Ross says. Chandler, however, is uncharacteristically quiet. Joey picks up a box and goes out the door. Then just as quickly he rushes back in and hugs Chandler from behind. Chandler smiles and then walks into his room.

Monica tells her parents that she's Richard's Twinkie.

At Jack's party that weekend, a family friend comes into the kitchen while Monica is helping her mother to announce that Richard has "some twenty-year-old Twinkie in the city." "Oh, so Richard's shopping in the junior section?" her mother chimes in. "She's probably got the IQ of a napkin," As they go at it, Monica shrinks into a teeny-tiny Twinkie ball.

Richard and Monica rendezvous in the bathroom. "I'm a Twinkie," she wails. "I'm a hero," he shrugs, referring to the very different reaction of the men. Once again he suggests that they should tell her parents. "Okay," Monica says. "Let's tell yours first." He would consider it, he says, if they weren't dead.

Richard makes his exit, but Judy is right outside the door. She sashays into the bathroom before Monica can slip out. Monica hides behind the shower curtain, hoping this will be brief, but then her father comes in. "What do you think about Richard and this twenty-year-old?" Judy asks him. He says he's never seen Richard so happy, that it's like a scene from *Cocoon*. In fact, Jack reports, Richard told him that he thinks he's falling in love. Monica is overjoyed at this revelation until her parents suddenly start to get intimate. She cringes in horror while they make out.

Back in the kitchen, Judy suggests to Richard that his son might be a potential match for Monica. There is some more cringing and then suddenly Monica blurts it out, "Actually Mother, I'm seeing someone." Ross makes a move for the door. Boy, does he not want to be around for this. Judy is miffed. Isn't that always the way, she says, the mother the last to know. "He's a doctor," Monica begins brightly. "A real doctor?" her mother asks. "No, a doctor of meat." Monica snaps. She stops herself, then continues, "Of course a real doctor." And that real doctor happens to be standing right beside her. "Jaaaaaccck," her mother wails. "This is the best relationship I've been in," she tells them both earnestly. Like they care. Into this happy domestic scene march the other birthday celebrants bearing Jack's birthday cake.

"It was crazy what happened with the studio audience when Tom Selleck hit the stage. It was like The Beatles with the screaming and the applause. We had to reshoot his entrance after the audience had gone home on all the shows he did with us."

MICHAEL LEMBECK

THE ONE WHERE
Eddie Moves In

Joey misses living with Chandler, but Chandler has already hooked another roommate; and Phoebe realizes the dream of a lifetime when she stars in a video of "Smelly Cat".

Director:
Michael Lembeck
Writer:
Adam Chase

JOEY HAS EVERYONE OVER TO SHOW OFF HIS FANCY new apartment. Everyone except Chandler, that is. Ross says he couldn't come because he had a … Thing. Joey gets the picture. Chandler obviously hasn't forgiven him yet for abandoning him to live the life of a big deal soap opera actor. But the truth is that Chandler misses Joey like crazy – so much so that he's started talking to his fuzzy puppy house slippers.

At the coffeehouse the next day, Joey tells Monica and Phoebe that he's not all that happy living alone. Like, for instance, he thought he'd like being alone with his thoughts. But it turns out that

> **"Okay, that's it! He just comes in here … Mr. Johnny New Eggs with his moving mail, and his, 'see ya, pals' and … nobody likes two different kinds of eggs equally. You like one better than the other, and I want to know which."**
>
> *– Joey –*

— 59 —

Believe it or not, Eddie seemed normal in the beginning.

he doesn't have as many thoughts as you'd think. The truth is he'd like to move back in with Chandler. Monica and Phoebe convince him to at least give it a try.

At the same time, however, Ross and Rachel are urging Chandler to face the fact that he and Joey are over as roommates. Joey is firmly entrenched in his new apartment, they tell him gently. He's even decorated. So Chandler takes the plunge and recruits a new roommate – a guy named Eddie he met in the ethnic foods department of a supermarket.

Screwing up his courage, Joey finally stops by Chandler's to broach the subject of their moving back in together. But instead of a touching reunion, Joey is met with the surreal sight of Eddie cooking breakfast while Chandler reads the paper. After an awkward round of introductions, Eddie splits. "He just comes in here with his Johnny New Eggs," Joey explodes. "Whose eggs do you like better, his or mine?"

On a happier note, Phoebe has been discovered by an agent who wants her to do a video of "Smelly Cat". But as the gang watches the finished product, it's clear to everyone (everyone but Phoebe) that the impressive singing voice coming out of Phoebe's mouth isn't hers. "Now I can hear what you hear when I'm singing," she says in total awe of herself. "I am sorry, but I am incredibly talented." It takes a while but eventually she realizes that she's been used. "You are not going to believe this," she tells the guys a few days later, "but that's not me singing on the video! That poor woman, the Voice Woman – she's so talented, but she doesn't have the right look. She's like one of those animals at the pound that no one wants 'cause she's not pretty. You know what? She's Smelly Cat!"

In the meantime, all is not well with Chandler and Eddie. For one thing, Eddie doesn't like foosball – which immediately makes him suspect. Far worse though is the unsettling fact that he doesn't like *Baywatch*, which he dismisses as "just a lot of pretty people running on the beach." Chandler tries to convince him that in and of itself is the brilliance of the show, but Eddie's not interested. He would rather just go to his room and read. And so, on opposite ends of town, Joey and Chandler sit in front of their TVs and watch the pretty people of *Baywatch* alone, together.

It's a dream come true. Phoebe lays down the vocal for "Smelly Cat" in the recording studio. (Or does she?)

Dr. Ramoray Dies

Joey gets fired from Days of Our Lives; *Monica tells Richard how many guys she's been with; and Chandler has gone from thinking Eddie's a little weird, to being positive he's a psycho.*

Director:
Michael Lembeck
Story:
Alexa Junge
Teleplay:
Michael Borkow

YOU WOULD HAVE THOUGHT THAT EDDIE WOULD BE a great roommate for Chandler – seeing as how he's a kind of urban hipster Chandler wouldn't have to explain his jokes to. But it turns out that Eddie's a secret psycho. Especially on the subject of his old girlfriend Tillie – who as he puts it – "reached into his chest, ripped out his heart and smeared it all over his life." Then when Tillie shows up one day to return Eddie's fish tank, he decides that she's had sex with Chandler. "She came over for, like, two minutes, dropped the fish tank, and left," Chandler yells. But Eddie's not through. Next he accuses him of killing his fish, Buddy.

Joey gets fired from *Days of Our Lives*. And it's his fault. He mis-speaks himself in an interview – his first – to *Soap Opera Digest* where he claimed to write a lot of his own lines. "Write this, Jerkweed," one of the old soap writers sniggered, as he pushed Joey's character down an elevator shaft.

Joey is so bummed he can't bear to tell anybody the truth. The gang only finds out because they happen to be watching as Dr. Ramoray takes the plunge. Concerned about him, they rush over to his fancy new apartment and bang on the

> **"I don't know. When I was little, I wanted to be a veterinarian. But then I found out you had to stick your hands into cows and stuff."**
>
> *– Joey –*
>
> *weighing his alternatives to his career in acting*

door. He pretends he's not there, but then Monica yells that she's really got to pee, and Joey lets them in. He tells them he was hoping nobody would notice he wasn't on the show and he could just go on being Dr. Ramoray forever.

(Above) **Phoebe tells Richard she likes him best of all Monica's many, many boyfriends.** (Right) **Rachel and Monica play paper-rock-scissors for the one and only condom – while Ross and Richard wait not at all patiently.**

Phoebe tells Richard that of all the men Monica has been with – and there have been a LOT – he's her favorite. Richard is flattered – sort of. Later when he and Monica are alone, he asks her just how many is a LOT. "You first," Monica dodges. Richard says, "Two." Monica's figure isn't that low, but it's totally manageable, Richard says – to her relief. Now she wants to go back to that two-number. She really can't believe it could be so low, because, well, "Have you looked at you lately?" He tells her he married his high school sweetheart and they were together for 30 years. And now he's with her. "But wait a minute," she says, "if you've only been with two women in your life, don't you have a lot of wild oats to sew?" Then she stops to think: "Is that what I am … an oat?" Not really, he explains, "I've only slept with people I've loved." Does that mean …? Yeah, it does.

The whole concept of "how many" makes Ross start to wonder; how many has Rachel … you know? She knows how many he's been with: "Carol and Julie and now … you." "There aren't that many," Rachel begins "Billy Dreskin, Pete Carney, and, Barry, and, oh, Paolo." But that almost doesn't count, since it was just meaningless animal sex. Ross starts to obsess over that painful concept until Rachel grabs him by the shoulders and says, "I'm not going to lie to you; it was good with Paolo, but as good as it was, what we have is so much better … This is the best I've ever had." Till now, Ross announces – and pulls her down on the bed. Wait, she says…

Monica and Rachel meet in the bathroom where both are frantically searching for that most necessary sexual accessory – a condom – only to discover that there's only one. After heated negotiation, they end up playing paper-rock-scissors and Rachel wins. "Fine, go have sex," Monica fumes. "They're doing it tonight," she tells Richard as she stomps past him into her room. "We'll do it tomorrow."

> "They came down on us about the condom thing in 'Dr. Ramoray Dies' where Monica and Rachel have the fight in the bathroom."
>
> MICHAEL CURTIS
>
> "We thought we were giving such a great message. When you think of friends, you think of responsible sex."
>
> GREG MALINS

Eddie Won't Go

The women fall under the spell of a self-help book; Joey gets the bills for the expensive stuff he bought when he was still Dr. Drake Ramoray; and Chandler gets Eddie to move with a creative mind-jam.

Director:
Michael Lembeck
Writers:
Michael Curtis & Gregory Malins

EDDIE IS STARTING TO SCARE CHANDLER. HE'S BEEN sitting in the dark watching him sleep and hallucinating trips to Las Vegas they haven't taken. He's also taken to dehydrating fruit – which isn't so bad – until he starts on water balloons. Chandler tells him he's got to move, to get out … now! "Hannibal Lechter?" he says. "Better roommate than you." But Eddie doesn't get the message. He still thinks they're the best of friends.

The women have discovered a book about female self-empowerment called *Be Your Own Windkeeper*. It's not exactly a feminist book. That's not really their thing. It's more a mystical belief-system that views women as goddesses. Actually, it's a bunch of gibberish is what it is. But they feel that it speaks to their very souls. Or as Rachel says, "This book could've been called *Be Your Own Windkeeper, Rachel*." At one of their discussion groups, Phoebe claims that she's never allowed a lightning bearer to take her wind. Monica and Rachel remind her about the puppet guy who she totally let wash his feet in the pool of her inner power. No doubt about it, these goddesses have a long way to go.

"'Envelope one of two.' That can't be good."
– Joey opens his charge card bill.

Chandler tells
Eddie he
moved out a
year ago.

Joey has recovered somewhat from the shock of losing his job as Dr. Drake Ramoray on *Days of Our Lives*. In fact, he's pretty upbeat about getting something else. But the only thing he's been offered is a two-line role as a cab driver on *Another World*. His agent, Estelle, assures him that the roles come and they go. He'll get something. But in the meantime, he should take this quickie. Like she told Al Menzer and His Pyramid of Dogs, "Take any job you can get and don't pee on the floor." Joey has too much pride. Or too much something. But he changes his mind when he gets back to his fancy apartment and finds a very scary charge card bill. "Envelope one of two," he says to Ross as he opens it, "that can't be good." "What were you thinking?" Ross chastises him as he stares at the bill in horror. Well, Joey explains, he was decorating his apartment and he made a few, you know, impulse buys. Joey doesn't know what he's going to do. Ross says, you're going to take the cab-driver part, that's what. You owe eleven hundred dollars to I Love Lucite.

Chandler is so scared of Eddie he's now sleeping on the sofa at Monica and Rachel's. He's got to get Eddie out. His sanity is at stake. But even though Eddie says, yeah, okay, fine when Chandler gives him another ultimatum, he continues playing with his dehydrated fruit. And then one night, as Chandler is sitting at Central Perk with Monica, Rachel and Phoebe – Eddie suddenly appears at the window holding a decapitated mannequin head. Eddie comes in and tells Chandler excitedly that they can turn the head upside down and use it for dip at their next party. Phoebe doesn't know what it is about Eddie, but she's starting to like him.

Ultimately, Chandler plays the situation like a champ. The next time Eddie comes home, he finds his stuff in boxes downstairs. And then when Chandler opens the door of the apartment, Eddie sees Joey settled comfortably in his Lazy Boy. What's going on, Eddie wants to know. Well, Chandler explains, you moved out a long time ago and Joey moved back in. You remember, don't you? Oh yeah, Eddie says.

"Talk about honest acting — Matt is amazing. There's such a kind of boldness about him. He's totally unflappable and so willing to do whatever you ask — including things that can't possibly work. And he's got the biggest heart of any human being. He's like the Tin Man in *The Wizard of Oz*."

MARTA KAUFFMAN and DAVID CRANE

2/9/96

19.
(I/H)

GUNTHER IS HILARIOUS IN THIS SCENE. CAN WE GIVE HIM MORE STUFF?
— MC

SCENE H

INT. COFFEE HOUSE - A BIT LATER (DAY 3)
(Joey, Gunther)

JOEY ENTERS AND CROSSES TO THE COUNTER. HE'S STILL BUMMED.

                          JOEY
          Hey, Gunther. Gimme a lemonade to
          go.

                          GUNTHER
          Lemonade? You okay, man?

                          JOEY
          Aah, career stuff. I don't know if
          you heard, but they killed off my
          character on the show.

                          GUNTHER
          That's too bad. How'd they do it?

                          JOEY
          I fell down an elevator shaft.

                          GUNTHER
          Aw, that sucks. I was buried in an
          avalanche.

                          JOEY
          Wh-what?

3AM Challenge

$3600

FOR SCOTT SILVERI TO EAT THE GIANT CAN OF BAKED BEANS

GREG - $200
Adam - $900
Ira - $300
Borkow - $200
MC - $100
David - $200
Marta - $200
Seth - $100
Wil C. - $150
_____
$2350

$1250 to go!

"We're very proud of James Michael Tyler who plays Gunther because we picked him out of the extras in the background at the coffee-house. We gave him a line and he killed with it. Then we gave him a bigger line and he killed with that. Now people are recognizing him on the street. And he's got his SAG card."

MICHAEL CURTIS

Old Yeller Dies

Director:
Michael Lembeck
Story:
**Michael Curtis &
Gregory Malins**
Teleplay:
Adam Chase

Ross moves a little too fast for Rachel. Richard is crushed when he discovers that Joey and Chandler think of him as a father figure. And Phoebe gets a tear-soaked education in sad movies.

ROSS IS FEELING LEFT OUT BECAUSE HE KEEPS missing all of baby Ben's Firsts. The first time he pulled himself up. The first time he waved bye-bye. Things have got to change. Nervously he tells Susan and Carol that he wants more time with his son. But he's barely gotten the words out before they've pelted him with affirmatives. They're definitely ready for a break. More time with Ben will also allow Rachel to get to know him better. She hasn't been around babies all that much. She's doesn't even know how to hold him. ("Like a football," Ross instructs her.)

That Ross ... he's every woman's dream. Except, of course, his ex-wife the lesbian. Oh, and Rachel. She feels positively claustrophobic when he reels off his precisely charted plans for their future. Like, for instance, he knows where they're going to live, how many children they'll have, what sex they'll be and in what order they'll be born. (And their names.) "One minute I'm holding Ben like a football," she wails, "the next I know I've got two kids, I'm living in Scarsdale and worrying about the taxes. You've planned out the next 20 years of our lives and we've only been dating for six weeks ... I don't want to

have my whole life decided for me. That's what I had with Barry, that's one of the reasons I left." Ross can accept that but he tells her she'd better face up to the idea that no matter what, they're going to end up together.

Monica wants Chandler and Joey to hang out with Richard more, to try and think of him as one of the gang. They tell her they really like him and he's a cool guy and all, but he's old. Monica asks them to give him a chance, if for no other reason, than to do it for her. And who knows, maybe if they invite him to the Knicks game, he might let them drive his Jaguar. He does and they do – hit it off, that is – so much so that Richard ends up spending more and more time across the hall. Monica tells him not to feel obligated, but he tells her that, far from it, he's crazy about the guys. For one thing, they don't begin every conversation with "You know who just died shoveling snow?"

Everybody is getting along great until the day that Chandler and Joey tell him how much cooler he is than their own dads. "You guys see me as a *dad*?" Richard asks, clearly crushed. Uh-oh. Chandler quickly (and lamely) attempts some damage control.

"When we say dad, we mean buddy, we mean pal," he improvises. "Seriously. Joey is my dad. Monica is my dad …."

Somehow, Phoebe has managed never to see the conclusion of the Disney classic *Old Yeller* and she doesn't have a clue as to how it ends. In fact, she doesn't have a clue about any sad movies because her mother, who was always very protective, always turned off movies with unhappy endings. That is, she did until she committed suicide. Phoebe realizes that she's missed out on a whole genre of movie-related emotions and sets out to get current. She rents *Brian's Song* and *Bang the Drum Slowly*, but by the time she's gotten through them, she's come to the conclusion that the world is an ugly place filled with hurt and disease and dying baseball players. Monica suggests that she watch *It's a Wonderful Life* and her faith in mankind will be restored. But Phoebe's not falling for that one. Just last night she watched another film with an upbeat title and it turned out to be a total downer. It was called *Pride of the Yankees* and the lead guy had Lou Gehrig's disease. "He *was* Lou Gehrig," Richard tells her, "Didn't you sort of see that coming?"

Rachel feels bad for Old Yeller, but that's nothing compared to her reaction to Ross's precisely charted plans for their future.

The Bullies

Director:
Michael Lembeck

Writers:
**Sebastian Jones
& Brian Buckner**

Ross and Chandler stand up (eventually) to two bullies in a contest for sofa rights at Central Perk; Monica ends up working in a Fifties theme restaurant after blowing her stash playing the stock market, and Phoebe tracks down her birth-father's second family and bonds with her spooky half-brother.

"But I need it. Otherwise, I'm going to have to take that horrible diner job. I don't want to have to wear flame-retardant boobs!"

– Monica –

CHANDLER AND ROSS ARE ROUSTED FROM THEIR USUAL sofa spot at Central Perk by two (large) Wall Street types – who take offense at one of Chandler's little jests. As Ross pulls Chandler away, one of them steals his baseball cap.

"Mean guys stole my hat," Chandler whimpers to the gang when they get home. "They were bullies." Ross says, "Mean bullies." Ross gets a comforting hug from Rachel. Chandler gets a hug from no one – which depresses him even more. Joey offers to go back to the coffeehouse and liberate his hat. "Forget it," Chandler pouts, "they've probably already stripped it and sold it for parts by now."

Meanwhile, Monica is so bored with being out of work that she's actually been watching the ticker on the business channel. One of the stocks has her initials "MEG", she explains, and it makes her happy when it goes by. Phoebe is seeing signs too – signs that point to her long-lost father. "Like when I was walking over here today," she explains, "I passed a buffet – which is my father's last name. And they were serving franks – which is his first name minus the "S" at the end. Coincidence? I don't think so."

Monica interviews for a job as a short order chef in a Fifties theme restaurant, where she would have to wear a campy waitress costume and dance in the "show". Is this any kind of job for someone who was a sous chef at Café des Artistes? Monica thinks not. There's just one little problem: she only has $127 left to her name. She starts to panic, and then happens to notice that her initials, er, her stock has gone up two points. That's it! She'll play the stock market to make the rent. And before breakfast the next day, she has made $17 on "CHP" and "ZXY." "What happened to 'MEG'?" Rachel asks. "Oh, I've moved on. My motto is 'Get out before they go down.'" Joey notes that that is so not his motto. Of course, it's only a matter of days before Monica has blown all her profits and more.

Joey and Rachel go along with Phoebe when she drives up to see her birth-father in upstate New York. But just as she's about to knock on the door, she's attacked by the family's demented little dog. Phoebe decides that this is a very bad sign – "you know, the beast at the threshold and all." They agree to pack it in and head back to the city. But as Phoebe steps down on the gas, the car is jolted by a dog-sized bump in the road. "What was that?" she asks tremulously. "I'm guessing," Joey says gently, "the threshold's clear now."

The dog pulls through and Phoebe returns it to her father's family. After handing it over it to the frowsy woman (guest star Larraine Newman) who answers the door, Phoebe timidly asks for Frank. "Fra-a-ank!" the woman yells and a dorky teenaged boy ambles out. Phoebe says oh, no, she meant, uh, Frank Sr. "He went out for groceries," the woman says, "four years ago." The kid wants to know how she knows his dad. "I don't really," she answers, "just genetically. He's kind of my dad too." She asks if he ever talked about her. "No," the kid says, "but he didn't really talk about anything – except stilts. He loved stilts."

Back at Central Perk, Ross and Chandler are determined to sit on their sofa and drink their coffee and then get the hell out. Too late, the bullies are back. No way to avoid it: they're going to have to fight. But while they negotiate the ground rules, two really bad guys run by and steal their stuff. Without stopping to think, Ross and Chandler team up with the bullies and run them down. High fives all around. (But don't get the idea that this means they're going to be friends.)

Over on Seventh Avenue, Monica, the former Wall Street Whiz and sous chef at Café des Artistes, is dancing on the counter of the Moondance Diner in a frowzy blonde wig, cat-eye glasses and very large flame-retardant boobs.

Michael Lembeck stages the non-fight between Chandler, Ross and the two bullies.

I'll Be There For You

It's the catchiest, most radio-worthy TV theme song since "(Hey, Hey) We're The Monkees". Just try and get it out of your mind (not that you'd want to). The Friends' *theme song, "I'll Be There For You," has accomplished something only two or three TV show theme songs ever have; it's not only achieved hit status, it's become a pop classic.*

STARTING WITH THE VERY DELIBERATE HOMAGE TO the apotheosis of pop – the Liverpool Sound – the song was a carefully crafted component of the *Friends* phenomenon masterminded by the show's creators. "I grew up on The Monkees and The Beatles and was very influenced by that stuff for 'I'll Be There For You,'" says Michael Skloff, one of the song's composers and the husband of producer, Marta Kauffman. According to Skloff, early models for the song were The Beatles' "Paperback Writer" and "I Feel Fine." The content of the song lyrics was shaped by the show's writer-creators, Kauffman and David Crane. And then, music maven Kevin S. Bright brought in the brilliant pop lyricist Allee Willis to spin the lyrics. Bright also recruited the talented pop-rock duo, The Rembrandts.

The song did what all good theme songs are supposed to do: it set up the dynamic of the show. (Not in quite as much detail as the *Gilligan* theme, but you got a clear idea of who and what were to come.) Interestingly, the now-famous montage of the show's cast dancing and mugging and making like The Beatles in *A Hard Day's Night* almost didn't make it on to the small screen. At that time, the networks were phasing out opening sequences, but producer Kevin Bright was granted an exemption to test a super-short montage, and the rest is TV history.

The original version of the song was little more than a riff – only 45 seconds long. But shortly into the show's run, disc jockeys around the country began taping the song off television and playing it on the air. Obviously the public was ready for more – which led to its expansion into a full-length version with additional lyrics by Marta Kauffman and David Crane.

"I'll Be There for You" can now be heard on the *Friends* soundtrack album, which also includes contributions from R.E.M., Lou Reed, k.d. lang, Joni Mitchell, Hootie and the Blowfish, Toad the Wet Sprocket, and more. A second soundtrack album will be released some time early next year.

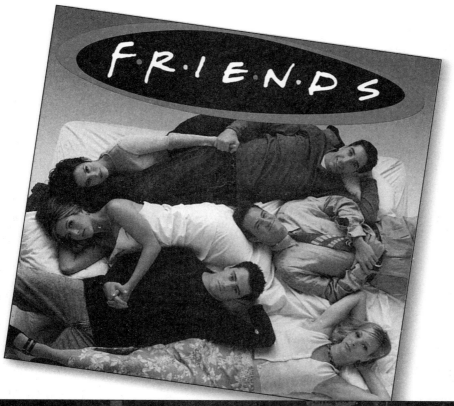

The *Friends* theme song goes gold.

Lisa Kudrow

"Oh my god, can that woman act! Who knew Phoebe had depth? We didn't."
Marta Kauffman

"When you write lines for a character, you always hear them in your head – but Lisa will always find something you never could have imagined."
David Crane

Yes they really *are* friends. Lisa Kudrow and Courteney Cox get the giggles during a rehearsal.

SHE IS *FRIENDS*' RESIDENT FLAKE, A GOOD-HEARTED air-head who is somewhat mentally challenged. But in one of *Friends*' more entertaining off-screen twists, Phoebe Buffay's real life counterpart – Lisa Kudrow – is a Brain.

Kudrow was well on her way to becoming a doctor and medical researcher after graduating from Vassar College. After college, she earned a credit on a breakthrough medical study on cluster headaches. So, how smart is she? Let's just say that her nickname at school was "Einstein" and leave it at that. Who knows? Had she stuck with her original game plan, she might've been responsible for a major medical breakthrough. But fortunately for mankind, Lisa Kudrow became an actress.

Lisa describes herself as "JAP-py" (as in Jewish American Princess) and it's true that she is a doctor's daughter who was born and raised in the heart of Valley Girl country – Encino, California, an upscale suburb of Los Angeles. While not exactly wealthy, it can safely be said that Lisa lived a privileged life while growing up.

Lisa wasn't one of those kids who sat around dreaming about being a movie star. In fact, the closest she got to performing as a child was throwing a rag over her head and lip-synching to the soundtrack of *Fiddler on the Roof* for her schoolmates. But, like many a funny kid who got laughs at the dinner table, Lisa was cheered on by her family. "I kept feeling like I was getting encouragement. Like, 'Oh you're good at this.' And it had a profound impact on me."

Even so, Lisa seemed destined to follow in the footsteps of her father, the eminent headache authority Dr. Lee Kudrow. She was a bookworm in primary school, an A student throughout high school, and a pre-med, then biology major at prestigious Vassar College in upstate New York. Kudrow graduated in 1985, fully intending to continue her research. Her interest in medicine stemmed from the family's genetic predisposition toward headaches. It was Dr. Kudrow's own cluster headaches – painful attacks that occur in series – that got the internist's research going in the first place.

But back to Lisa's trek toward stardom. In 1985, the same year Lisa graduated from Vassar, her brother's close friend, comic Jon Lovitz, landed a spot in the Not Ready for Prime Time Players at *Saturday Night Live*. Lovitz's new job impressed Lisa, and awakened acting ambitions until then buried deep inside her.

Lovitz recommended that she audition for the Groundlings, the Los Angeles improvisational comedy troupe that had honed his talents as well as those of Phil Hartman, Paul Reubens (Pee Wee Herman), and Larraine Newman among others. A few months of acting lessons got Lisa up to speed.

LISA KUDROW

TELEVISION:

BOB	Recurring	CBS/Paramount
MAD ABOUT YOU	Guest Star	NBC/Tristar
FLYING BLIND	Guest Star	FBC/Paramount/Viacom
COACH	Guest Star	ABC/Universal
MURDER IN HIGH PLACES	Co-Star (MOW)	NBC/NBCP
LIFESTORIES	Guest Star	ABC/Ohlmeyer
LIFE GOES ON	Co-star	ABC/Warner Bros.
NEWHART (Final Episode)	Guest Star	CBS/MTM
CHEERS	Guest Star	NBC/Paramount
ROOM FOR TWO	Co-Star	ABC/Warner Bros.
ON THE TELEVISION	Ensemble	Nickelodeon
ONLY TEMPORARY (Pilot)	Lead	NBC/Spelling Prods.

FEATURES:

Heat of Passion	Concorde	Director:	Rodman Flender
Dance with Death	Concorde		Chuck Moore
The Unborn	Concorde		Rodman Flender
Impulse	Warner Bros.		Sondra Locke

THEATER:

GROUNDLINGS	Main Company	Groundling Theater
TRANSFORMERS	Improvisation	Up Front Theater
LADIES ROOM by Robin Schiff,		Theater on the Square
Dir., Kim Friedman		
LADIES ROOM by Robin Schiff		Tiffany Theater
Dir., Kim Freidman		
MAPS FOR DROWNERS by Neal Landau		Tiffany Theater
Dir., Allison Liddy		
GIRLS CLUB	Ensemble	Groundling Theater
Dir., Cynthia Szigeti		

She very easily could have become a doctor or a medical researcher, but fortunately for mankind, Lisa Kudrow decided to become an actress.

Guest star Charlie Sheen is nervous about tonight's shoot. Lisa Kudrow isn't. Can you tell?

member of the Los Angeles comedy scene, one who spent her nights performing and her days auditioning for sitcom and movie guest shots. She won a few small parts in low-budget movies, and a role in a local theater production called *The Ladies Room*. Her first TV job of note was the role of the girlfriend of Woody Harrelson's character on an episode of *Cheers*. Similar brief bits on *Coach* and *Newhart* followed, but it was 1993 before she finally secured the breakthrough role as Ursula on *Mad About You*. Her hilarious comedic turns as the warped waitress were a hit not only with audiences but with NBC – which encouraged her to audition for some of its sitcom pilots. And in fact, she was briefly cast as the talk-show producer Roz on *Frasier*, only to be replaced at the last minute by the more believably methodic Peri Gilpin. Never-theless, the network was set on providing a vehicle for her unique talents, and she was cast in *Friends* not long after.

Kudrow continued to play Ursula on *Mad About You* while at the same time playing Phoebe, whom the *Friends'* producers cleverly birthed as Ursula's twin sister. "We decided to make a virtue out of this," says producer David Crane, "rather than having it seem like a ridiculous coincidence." Eventually Ursula herself would make an appearance on *Friends*, where she had a little fling with Joey during the first season, and then again a year later when she became the object of an inept stalker who kept confusing her with Phoebe. (When Ursula appears with Phoebe during her occasional visits to *Friends*, Lisa Kudrow's sister, artist Helene Sherman, serves as a double for over-the-shoulder shots.) Phoebe often mentions Ursula, although not in the friendliest of terms, since she and her twin don't exactly get along.

In l995 and 1997, Kudrow won Emmy nominations for Outstanding Supporting Actress in a Comedy Series for her work on *Friends*. (Not bad for someone who took on acting as a second career.) In l996, she did a hilarious turn in the Albert Brooks' comedy *Mother* and the following year she co-starred

(Kids, don't try this at home.) And it wasn't long before Kudrow was accepted into the Groundlings' exclusive little club. "When I began doing improvisation," she recalls now, "it turned me from a kind of judgmental, fearful person into a very open and trusting person. That type of person may be less funny than a judgmental, angry person – but it's an easier person to be."

During the troupe's weekly shows, she developed a gaggle of characters that won her a sizeable following – most notably a bumbling doctor type who lectured in incomprehensible medicalese. Within a few years, Kudrow was a well-known

> "Lisa has created this character that is so positive — who loves trees and animals and ants and life!"
>
> MARTA KAUFFMAN

Phoebe's look as designed by Debra McGuire is sexy-slash-bohemian.

with Mira Sorvino in the uproarious *Romy and Michelle's High School Reunion* – playing a character spun off the little part she'd played in the stage production of *The Ladies Room*.

You could say that Lisa Kudrow is the Friend with the most experience in what is sometimes referred to as the Real World. She is the only cast member who is married – to a civilian. And she is also the only one who's got a great back-up job. But let's hope she doesn't go back to the lab any time soon. A good belly-laugh is nature's best medicine and Lisa Kudrow prescribes that better than almost anyone.

Costume design by Debra McGuire

Two Parties

Director:
Michael Lembeck

Writer:
Alexa Junge

Rachel's parents are splitting up and it's not pretty. The gang tries to keep them apart when they both show up for Rachel's surprise birthday party.

(Top right)
See, he's not so scary. Ron Liebman (Dr. Green) entertains Jennifer Aniston during a break on "The One With Two Parties."
(Below)
Rachel does her best to keep her father out of the "staging area" across the hall.

NO MATTER WHERE RACHEL'S PARENTS GO THESE days, they are constantly at each other's throats – even at her sister's college graduation, where they got into such a noisy brawl, Bishop Tutu had to shush them. Rachel knows she's supposed to be a grownup, but her parents' break-up is making her feel like a little kid.

The gang hopes to cheer her up with a surprise birthday party. Naturally, Monica wants to do something special, but the others are thinking more along the lines of pizza and beer. Monica doesn't push it, but she has no intention of settling for anything less than Martha Stewartesque perfection. And from the looks of it, she's come pretty close.

But into Monica's pretty fantasy pops a little unexpected surprise – Rachel's father, the dyspeptic Dr. Green. Ordinarily, this wouldn't be a problem. It's just that Rachel's mother is due to arrive any minute too. Monica and Phoebe do their best to discourage Dr. Green from staying, short of slamming the door in his face. Once he sees that there's a party for his little girl, nothing can make him budge.

When Rachel's mother knocks at the door a few minutes later, Joey quickly pulls Dr. Green into the bedroom. Phoebe then pulls Rachel's baffled mother into the bathroom. Next, Monica orders Chandler and Joey to take Dr. Green over their place – which they do, explaining that that's where the "real" party is happening. As people start to arrive, Chandler takes advantage of the situation by directing all the women into his apartment.

Later, Ross and Rachel return from a romantic dinner and make their entrance into Party Number One as planned. But Rachel isn't nearly as surprised by the party as she is by the sight of her father across the hall at Party Number Two. Ross doesn't want to get caught up in this craziness. "I say we just put them together and if they can't deal with it, who cares?" he says. Rachel says she does.

As the night wears on, the two parties go in very different directions. Monica's soirée is like a remedial workshop for the socially stiff – whereas, over at the boys' place, it's a funfest with dancing and pick-up volleyball and, oh yeah, Rachel's Dad. Monica's guests are desperate to sneak out to the good party. Phoebe takes pity on them and does what she can.

Rachel goes back and forth between the parties and her parents, listening patiently as they both mouth off about the other. Totally drained, she ends up in the hall venting to Chandler. She can see it all now, she tells him: her mother will get the house and her father will be in some condo that her sister will decorate with wicker.

Monica wants everyone to write their most embarrassing moment on a piece of paper...

In the meantime, Ross has been assigned the job of making sure Dr. Green doesn't come anywhere near Monica's party. He tries to make conversation but, as always, Dr. Green isn't interested. What he would be interested in is a scotch. Neat. No problem, Ross says. He'll just zip over to Monica's to whip that up. Dr. Green should stay put and not move a muscle. At Monica's, he then weirds out Mrs. Green by making himself the same cocktail her husband drinks. In the hall, Ross then runs into Dr. Green who's on his way in to get his eyeglasses and cigarettes. No! Ross yells – really loud. He'll get them. Mrs. Green then notices that Ross's eyeglasses look just like her husband's. And not only that, he smokes! Yes, yes he does, Ross tells her. He puts on Dr. Green's bifocals, sticks a cigarette in his mouth and heads for the door. Mrs. Green pulls Rachel aside and insists that she see a therapist. It's obvious that she's chosen a boyfriend who's exactly like her father.

When Rachel's parents end up leaving the parties at the same time, the guys manage to keep them from seeing each other by surrounding Dr. Green and moving him across the hall and then back down the stairs while Joey diverts Mrs. Green with a fiery goodnight kiss. "This is the best party I've been to in years!" she declares as she stumbles into the night in a blissful daze.

Rachel's mother insists that Rachel see a therapist because she's chosen a boyfriend who's exactly like her father.

"The One With Two Parties" Final Draft (3/8/96) 29.
(II/H)

PHOEBE (CONT'D)

When I do, walk quickly to the door

and don't look back.

RESET TO:

INT. JOEY AND CHANDLER'S - MOMENTS LATER
(Ross, Dr. Green)

ROSS AND DR. GREEN ARE STILL PAUSING. ROSS LAUGHS AT NOTHING. THEN:

DR. GREEN

I think I need a drink.

ROSS

Let me. What can I get for you?

DR. GREEN

Scotch.

ROSS

You got it. I'll be back in ten seconds with your Scotch! On the rocks! In a glass!

DR. GREEN

Neat.

ROSS

Cool.

DR. GREEN

No, neat. As in "no rocks".

★ Call Doug
★ Call MOM
★ Call Anne Blanchard AT William MoRRis

Will Young people get THIS?

I FeeL OLD

you ARe OLD

"My favorite thing in 'The One With Two Parties' is Phoebe smuggling people out of Monica's party. The underground railroad concept is so hilarious to me. And she played it so well."

MARTA KAUFFMAN

"This was a very difficult episode to pin down — because, really, the show isn't about broad comedy. But we realized that we had to embrace the sheer farce of all the people sneaking around and yet somehow still combine it with the heart of the story — which played out between Rachel and Chandler in the hall."

DAVID CRANE

The One With

The Chicken Pox

Phoebe gets the chicken pox just as her dreamy sailor boy Ryan is due in for his bi-annual visit; and Chandler gets Joey a job as a computer processor and Joey becomes "Joseph," a phony suck-up who almost gets Chandler fired.

Director:
Michael Lembeck
Writer:
L. Brown Mandell

EVERY TWO YEARS, PHOEBE'S DASHING SUBMARINE guy Ryan (guest star Charlie Sheen) comes up for air to spend a romantic weekend all alone with her. But the day before his arrival, she catches chicken pox from Ross's baby son. Monica and Rachel do what they can to cover the blisters – but the overall effect is still zit city. "Look, Ryan's been underwater," Monica tells her. "He's gonna be glad you don't have barnacles on your butt."

But Phoebe's not taking any chances. When Ryan arrives, she greets him with her head covered by a long chiffon scarf. What's going on, he asks. Oh nothing, she says blithely, it's just that she has The Pox. "Small or chicken?" he inquires. Chicken, she answers, adding how desperately she hopes he's had them, since she'd forgotten how cute he is. Alas, no – he hasn't. But now that he's here, surely she can take off that spooky scarf. But just as she does, there's a huge bolt of lightning and a giant thunderclap which illuminates the room. Ryan screams like a baby. "See, I am scary," Phoebe cries. "You look lovely, lovely!" he assures her. And then he proves it by leaping across the coffee table and taking her in his arms. Phoebe says this is the most romantic disease she's ever had.

Joey is out of work as usual, so Chandler offers to get him a job as an entry-level computer processor. Joey can't imagine how he could pull that off, but Chandler tells him, you're an actor, just play the part. Now that Joey understands and within a matter of hours, he has transformed himself into Joseph – a family man with slicked-back hair and double-breasted suits. Joseph isn't exactly a whiz at the processing thing but he loves the people part of his job – like schmoozing with his co-workers about his boat and his wife Karen and their two little girls – Ashley and Brittany. "Wait a minute, wait a minute," Chandler explodes. "What are you doing?

Lisa Kudrow and Charlie Sheen during a break on the set of "The One With The Chicken Pox".

dropped the ball with the Lender project, Joey tells him, until Joseph told him that it was actually Chandler. That's it. Chandler has had it. He says that his character Chandy is going to have to fire Joey. That is, if he doesn't kill him first. Joey feels badly. He's going to miss Joseph an awful lot. He'd really grown to like him, not to mention his wife Karen – who was really hot.

Ryan's leave is over and he's bound for the old sardine can. Phoebe's disappointment is written all over her now unblemished face. There were so many things she had planned for them to do together. And there were so many things Ryan had had in mind. Oh well, she'll just have to wait for another two years.

(Above) **Ryan (guest star Charlie Sheen) and Phoebe can't stop scratching.** (Right) **Ryan tells Phoebe how beautiful she is, but his oven mitts are covering her ears.**

What are you doing?" Joey patiently explains that these little details are his character's back-story.

By the time we see Ryan and Phoebe again, his face is as blotchy as Phoebe's and their idea of a hot night is using their Monopoly hotels to rub on their itchy bodies. Monica tries to help by taping oven mitts on their hands. But then during the one time when Ryan takes Phoebe's face in his hands and tells how beautiful she is, she doesn't hear him because his mitts are covering her ears.

Back at the office, Joey rushes in to tell Chandler that he's in for trouble with his boss, Mr. Douglas. But why, Chandler asks, what happened? Okay, well, at first, Douglas thought that Joseph had

> "The studio audience loved Charlie Sheen – which was great because Charlie was scared to death to do a live shoot. He was like the Peter O'Toole character in My Favorite Year who says, 'I'm not an actor, I'm a Movie Star!' His brother Emilio Estevez stayed with him on the stage the whole time to give him support. As the night went on Charlie got looser and funnier and the laughs came faster and easier. By the end of the shoot, he was a total pro."
>
> MICHAEL LEMBECK

For GREG GRANDE
Date 5/29/96   Time _____ A.M./P.M.
WHILE YOU WERE OUT
M⸍ DAVID CRANE
Of
RE: S+P CONCERNS
THE ONE WITH
THE CHICKEN POX
Area Code   Number   Extension

TELEPHONED	✔	PLEASE CALL	✔
CAME TO SEE YOU		WILL CALL AGAIN	
WANTS TO SEE YOU		URGENT	
RETURNED YOUR CALL		SPECIAL ATTENTION	

Message
OVEN MITT DESIGN

CAN WE SEE PHOEBE'S MIDDLE FINGER WHEN SHE FLICKS OFF ROSS?

Signed

"The One With The Chicken Pox" Final Draft (3/29/96)

14.
(I/H)

JOEY

Yeah. Turns out our kids go to the same school. Small world, huh? *

CHANDLER

Weird world. Your kids?

JOEY

I figured my character has kids.

CHANDLER

There's no part of that sentence I don't need explained.

JOEY

Well, when you're acting, you need to think about stuff like that. My character, Joseph The Processing Guy, has two little girls, Brittany and Ashley. (CHUCKLING) Ashley copies everything Brittany does. *

CHANDLER

Sounds like they're just the dickens.

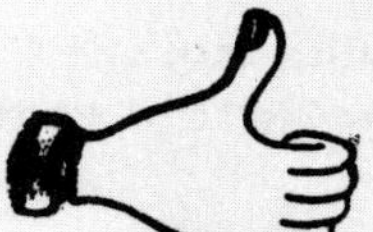

JOEY

They are. Joseph and Karen are thinking about having a third kid. (CONSIDERING THIS) You know what? They just did. *

I LOVE THIS DEEPLY!
D.C.

how about "Imaginary Kids will do that?"

Something about "imaginary sperm" here?

Barry And Mindy's Wedding

Director:
Michael Lembeck
Story:
Ira Ungerleider
Teleplay:
L. Brown Mandell

Monica tells Richard she wants to have children; Chandler has an online love affair; Rachel walks down the aisle at her Ex's wedding with the back of her skirt tucked into her underwear, and Joey tries to kiss every man in sight.

Barry tells Rachel that his family told everyone that she'd gone insane (from the syphilis) after she ran out on their wedding.

"We were all involved in one story [for "The One With Barry And Mindy's Wedding"] where Joey goes on an audition and gets called back and they ask him if he's circumcised, because he has to be to get the part. He lies and says he is."

GREG MALINS

"When it got killed, we had two hours to come up with a new story. We replaced it with one where Joey has auditioned for a part in a Warren Beatty movie and he has to kiss a man, so he tries to practise on Ross."

MICHAEL BORKOW

JOEY IS UP FOR A JUICY PART IN A BIG MOVIE, BUT the director doesn't think he's a good kisser. (Which, to Joey, is like saying that Mother Theresa isn't a good mother.) The problem is that he's got to kiss a guy – which, admittedly, he hasn't done all that much. No problem. He'll just practice on every guy he knows. He starts with Ross, who says "over my dead body." Joey then turns to Chandler who informs him that he'll be using Ross's dead body as a shield.

Besides, Chandler doesn't want to make out with anyone but his new cyber squeeze. Yes, he's having a torrid online romance with a fabulous mystery woman. Phoebe thinks he – and his little computer fling – couldn't be any cuter. And brave.

Think about it, she says, the person on the other end of that throbbing cursor could be 90 years old. Or have two heads. Or it could be a *guy*! Yeah, what if it's a BIG GIANT GUY? Phoebe suggests that he ask his pen pal some gender specific questions – like what method of birth control she uses. Chandler types the question. "My husband is sleeping with his secretary," she answers back. She's a woman all right. A married one. She begs to meet him, but what's the use? But Phoebe persists on her behalf. "What if the husband person is the wrong guy and you're the right guy?" Phoebe asks him. "You don't get chances like this all the time." All right, he'll do it.

Who ever said love is easy? Take Monica. She is completely swoony over Richard. It's like he couldn't be any more perfect. That is, if only he wanted children. It's not that he doesn't like them. He loves them. He *has* them. Grown ones. Of course, Monica wants kids more than anything in the world. "I *have* to have children," she tells him. "I just do." Fortunately, Richard understands. "If I have to," he says, "I'll do it all again." But Monica, straight arrow that she is, doesn't want to do it that way. So where does that leave them? Maybe nowhere.

Meanwhile, Rachel is going to Barry and Mindy's wedding and she is a wreck! After all, her last wedding with Barry was hers and everybody knows how *that* turned out. To make things worse, she's got to wear a frothy pink dress with big puffed sleeves that makes her look like Princess Bubble Yum. She hasn't been this nervous since the eighth grade when she tried to sing "Copacabana" in front of the entire school. So don't go, Ross tells her. But she *has* to go. She's the maid of honor and she promised Mindy. But more importantly, she has to be in a room with those people and show them that she finally feels good about herself. But hey, what's the worst that could happen? Well, she could walk down the aisle with the back of her skirt tucked into her panties and her backside completely exposed.

"It's not many women who would have the guts to come back here tonight," the Best Man says

raising his glass to her later that evening, "and even fewer who'd do it with their asses hanging out." Ross stands up to say a few – really lame – words in her defense. Humiliated, Rachel bolts for the door, only to turn and climb up on the stage. Trembling, she makes a weak little joke. What else is there to say? Rachel certainly doesn't know, so instead she begins to sing (what else?) "Copacabana."

Back at Central Perk, Chandler is a basket case as he awaits the arrival of Lady X. And then … she walks through the door.

OH MY GOD … it's Janice!

Monica and Richard dance before their Big Talk at Barry and Mindy's wedding.

GENERATION ECCH DEPT.

And now a show about six twentysomethings! They're single, they're attractive, they're witty, they're bonding, and they've got something great going for them: it's called Thursday night on NBC! The amazing thing is they claim it's all platonic and there's no hanky-panky going on between them. And the Pope was born in Guatemala!) Whatever they claim, we know them for what they really are--sex...

Hi, I'm **Shoey!** I'm a **hot hunk** on this show! I'm a **babe magnet!** My **interests?** I love **movies,** I love **sports,** and I love **myself!** Not necessarily in **that order!**

I'm **Chandelier!** I'm also a **babe magnet!** I'm a **wisecracking data processor!** Not a combination you find a **lot** of in the business world! I'm **great-looking** and **devastatingly funny,** yet I can't seem to **connect** with **women!** Like, I invite women back to my place for a little **wine, soft music,** and a series of **blistering put-down one-liners!** But for some reason this **doesn't** seem to **turn them on!**

I'm **Floss!** I'm **not** a **babe magnet!** But I have been **struck** by **lightning** three times! I'm the **whiner** of the show! Things have **not** gone **well** in **my life!** My **ex-wife** left me for a **lesbian lover!** I have a **crush** on **Regal** who **ignores me!** I have a **monkey** on my **back**— **literally!** I guess the only **good thing** in my life is that I'm allowed to **park** in "Handicapped" **spots!** Why? They've seen **my haircut!**

Who wants **pie à la mode?**

I **do!** And could you put some **ice cream** on **top?**

Does anyone have a **straw?**

What for?

Maybe we can let a **little air** out of Pheeble's **head!**

4   ARTIST: MORT DRUCKER   WRITER: JOSH GORDON

The Princess Leia Fantasy

Monica is torching for Richard; Janice gives Joey a pain; and Rachel tarts herself up as Ross's ultimate fantasy girl, but all he can see is his mother.

Director:
Gail Mancuso
Writers:
Michael Curtis & Gregory Malins

CHANDLER AND JANICE ARE BACK TOGETHER BUT Joey hopes that Chandler will end up dumping her like he did before. Joey doesn't hate her, he tells him, she's just, well, a lot to take. He thinks maybe it's a kind of a chemical thing. Like when she laughs, he just wants to rip his arm out and throw it at her.

Across the hall, Rachel asks Ross if he ever has any, you know, little fun fantasy type thoughts, because if he tells her what they are, she just might do them. "There is one thing. You know *Return of the Jedi*? Remember the scene with Jabba the Hut? Well Jabba has as his prisoner Princess Leia and she's wearing that gold sort of bikini thing that was really cool."

Not one to be shy, Janice tells Joey that a little bird told her that he hates her. It's not *that* bad, Joey says uncomfortably. No matter. Janice suggests that they try to get to know each other better by having "Joey and Janice's Day of Fun." Does it have to be a *whole* day? Joey winces. "Yes, because that's how long it takes to love me," Janice explains. Actually, Joey knows how long it takes all too well. He sleeps in the next room.

Rachel tells Monica and Phoebe all about Ross's *Star Wars* fixation, and is surprised to hear that Phoebe knows all about the Princess Leia fantasy. In fact she's done it a few times herself. Later when Phoebe pokes fun at Ross by holding two Leia-like dinner rolls on her ears, Ross is mortified. Women talk about these things all the time, Rachel protests. Well, men don't. What can Rachel say? Obviously, women are different. Okay then, he wants to know, did you tell Phoebe about The Night of Five Times. "That was with Carol not me," she reminds him. He knows, but it's still worth mentioning.

Poor Monica. She's absolutely shattered by the break-up with Richard. She can't sleep. She can't eat. She's even found herself collecting Richard's drain hair. She knows it's gross, but it's practically all she has left of him. (Or rather it was, until she dropped it into Ross's cereal bowl.) They all do what they can to pull her out of her depression, but the only thing that helps is when her dad tells her that Richard is a mess too.

Ross wants to know if Chandler is aware that women tell each other everything: "Stuff *you* like,

"Yuh, right. You look me in the eye and tell me, without blinking – no blinking – that you're not breaking up with her."

– Joey –

October 4, 1996

Mr. Kevin Bright
Ms. Marta Kauffman
Mr. David Crane
Executive Producers
Bright, Kauffman and Crane
Building 160, Suite 750
4000 Warner Boulevard
Burbank, California 91522

Dear Kevin, Marta, and David:

I must tell you how much my family and I enjoyed watching the season premiere of "Friends." The Princess Leia fantasy was great! Congratulations on a terrific series and a brilliant season premiere.

Sincerely,

George Lucas

GWL/am

DAVID'S TO DO LIST

- Table episode #13
- Re-write pilot for "Veronica's Closet"
- Notes on Writer's Draft of episode #14
- Send flowers to Jeffrey
- Watch cut of episode #11
- Resist panic
- Run-thru for episode #12
- Casting for Frank Jr's fiancee
- Call Mom with ratings
- Explain to Mom that ratings don't matter.
- Pitch episode #15 to NBC and Warner Bros.
- Break episode #17
- Convince Marta she has no problems with episode #16.
- Okay, panic

stuff *she* likes, technique, stamina, girth." Wait a minute. Girth? Chandler is suddenly alert. "Yes, girth," Ross says. Anyway, he tells him, Rachel says that us guys are really missing out by not sharing on an intimate level. Chandler says he's game, so long as they don't have to talk about girth. Ross starts the bidding with his Princess Leia, but Chandler definitely ups the ante. "You know when you're in bed with a woman," he begins "and you get all these mental images in your brain like of Elle MacPherson? And then all of a sudden your mom pops into your head and it's like Mom, get out of here. But then before you know it, you're … " Ross is shocked. "You're telling me you … with your *mom*? What is *wrong* with you?"

Joey tells Chandler that his day with Janice showed him that he could spend time with her without wanting her dead. Oh, and by the way, Ross told him about the thing with his mom and he wants him to know that it's no big deal. In fact, he does it too. Yeah, he always pictures Chandler's mom when he's having sex.

That night, Rachel does her Princess Leia. The hair. The gold bikini top. Everything's perfect. But then Ross gets a weird look on his face. "What's wrong?" she asks him. But how can he tell her that she's turned into his mother in Princess Leia drag. All he can say is, "I hate Chandler," he whimpers. "The bastard ruined my life."

"It's weird, but I don't want to throw this away. It's like all I have left of him … gross drain hair."

– Monica –

"Oh, that explains it, because she called me around 2 A.M. At first all I could hear were little squeaky sounds so I thought maybe it was a mouse or a possum – but then I thought 'Where would a mouse or a possum get the money to make a phone call?'"
– Phoebe

THE ONE WITH THE PRINCESS LEIA FANTASY

the Princess Leia Fantasy

"The One Without a Title"
7/25/96 Post Cut Pass Draft

41.
(II/T)

ROSS

Oh, yeah, sure.

CHANDLER

Do you ever have it where, like,
you're thinking of Elle MacPhereson —
or that girl at the Xerox place?

Some one less General?
i like

ROSS

With the belly button ring?

But it's okay to picture other's people's mom's Right?

CHANDLER

Yeah, and then, like, all of a
sudden, your mom pops into your
head, and you're like, "Mom, get
out of here." But now, of course,
it's the only thing you can think
about. [And you just know it's some
part of you that doesn't want you
to be happy or feel pleasure,] you
know? You know? You don't know.

CAN WE GO HOME YET?

So It's actually like you're Doing It w/your MOM?....You know?

↑ CAN'T SAY That

ROSS (BEAT)

Oh, my god! How could you tell me
that?

ROSS GETS A HORRIFIED LOOK ON HIS FACE.

CHANDLER

Well... You asked...

ROSS

I said "share", not "scare"! Wow!
You must never, ever tell anyone
this! I'm the most sensitive guy
you know, and I am so judging you.

X		O
	X	O
O	X	X

↑ WIL CHEATED. I WOULD HAVE WON.

ADAM

+

IRA

=

MICHAEL CURTIS

— 92 —

No One's Ready

Ross is giving a career-making speech at the museum tonight and he's taking the whole gang with him – that is, if they'll just get dressed!

Director:
Gail Mancuso
Writer:
Ira Ungerleider

THIS IS A BIG NIGHT FOR ROSS. HE'S SCHEDULED TO make a speech at a black-tie party at the museum. And all he asks is that everyone be on time. But of course, he arrives at Monica and Rachel's to find everyone acting the same as always. Joey and Chandler are fighting over who gets to sit in the comfy chair, and Rachel can't decide what she's going to wear, and Monica isn't even home yet. Oh great. Ross can see it coming. Disaster. Here it comes, walking down the street. Thankfully Phoebe arrives looking totally swanked out. "Now this is a person who is ready to go," Ross says as he hugs her gratefully. "Phoebe, you're my star." And she would've stayed that way, if the boys hadn't pelted her with hummus during their ongoing scuffle.

Rachel comes out of the bedroom holding up a dark suit. Does this look like something the girlfriend of a paleontologist would wear, she wonders? Ross thinks it's fine. Never mind, she's just remembered that this is the outfit that makes her calves look fat.

She's got the upper hand ... again. Rachel is sufficiently placated by Ross's heart-felt apology.

"Well, ever since I was yelled at and humiliated in front of my friends, I dunno. I'm just not in a museum-benefitty kind of mood."
– Rachel

"Look at me, I'm Chandler. Could I BE wearing any more clothes?"

– Joey–

"Hey thanks, guys, you were great too." The cast applauds the audience after shooting "The One Where No One's Ready."

Ross turns his attention to Chandler and Joey – who are now both sitting in the comfy chair. Chandler thinks he's winning because he's the one on top until Joey says it's starting to feel pretty good. When Joey finally leaves to go get dressed, he takes the chair cushions with him. But he's back in a flash, to thrust an accusing finger at Chandler. Where is all my underwear? Easy, he hid it. Ross tells him to just go without – like he always does. He can't, he explains, because he's wearing a rented tux and he's not going commando in another man's fatigues.

Monica finally shows up and Ross orders her to step on it. Sure, fine … but first she wants to check her phone messages. There's one from Phoebe and one from Ross and the third one is from Richard. Richard! "Is that an old or a new?" she shrieks. OLD OR NEW? It's bound to be old, the gang assures her. Still she can't stop herself from calling back. She tells Richard's answering machine that she got a message from him but if it's an old one to forget it. She plays it back and makes everyone listen to see if she sounds too crazy. She definitely does, but that doesn't matter after she hears the next message from a sexy sounding woman saying "thanks for yesterday". "I can't believe he's already seeing someone else!" Monica explodes. Maybe it's his sister or his daughter, someone suggests. Ross says she can find out later, but now she's got to get dressed.

Rachel comes out in a second outfit. But she's not sure which shoes to wear. Ross finally loses it and ends up balling her out with a vengeance. The next time Rachel comes out, she's dressed in her sweats. She will not be attending the ball.

Monica can't leave until she's called Richard's daughter Michelle. Happily, it only takes a quick hello to confirm that she's the sexy-message-girl. Incredibly relieved, Monica quickly hangs up. But then the phone rings. Apparently, Michelle has caller ID. Monica begs her not to tell her father, but she knows there's not much chance of that. So she ends up doing it herself. Unfortunately, she presses the wrong code when she's through and it records as his outgoing message. Ross tells her to get dressed.

Meanwhile, Chandler has managed to get his tux on and is actually ready to leave until Joey comes in the door wearing all of his clothes. That's it. Ross has had it. He doesn't care if any of them go. The only person he wanted to come with him isn't speaking to him and now his night is ruined anyway. Rachel forgives him and gets dressed in a flash. Ross has got two cabs waiting downstairs. It looks like they might actually make it on time.

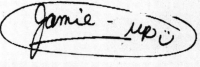

3633 Rolling Meadows Drive
Bedford, Texas 76021

4/21/96

Department of Public Relations
NBC
3000 W. Alameda
Burbank, CA 91523

Dear NBC:

Our son Walter L. Searcey, a Specialist in the US Army stationed in Bosnia, wrote us asking if we would copy and send some movies, as they now have both a TV and a VCR where is is camped. We began renting and copying today. I would love to send him "Friends", because he, nor anyone in his camp, have ever seen "Friends" as they were stationed in Baumholder, Germany before being shipped to Bosnia. I know Walter and the rest of his camp would love the series; however, the few copies that I have would be meaningless without the first few episodes. Is there any chance that NBC would send copies of all of the "Friends" episodes to Camp Lisa in Bosnia? Actually Walter is stationed in Serbia right next to Sebrenica, so if you sent it to Headquarters in Tusla, Walter would never see it. But to be fair, I know all of the members of Operation Joint Endeavor, regardless of where stationed, would love any of the Thursday night NBC programs.

Attached is Walter L. Searcey's address. I've no idea what his commander's name is, but I do know that all 600 at Camp Lisa share one TV and one VCR.

Who would've thought that missing *Friends* would be one of the toughest aspects of keeping the peace in Serbia in the spring of 1996? By the way, a full carton of *Friends* episodes was sent from Kevin Bright's office to Specialist Walter L. Searcey at Camp Lisa in Serbia with the compliments of the cast and crew.

The Jam

Director:
Kevin S. Bright

Writer:
Wil Calhoun

Joey regresses into jam heaven; Chandler tries to understand what it takes to be part of a couple and Monica contemplates motherhood without a man.

JOEY SPRAINS HIS ARM WHILE JUMPING ON HIS BED (alone). It's nothing serious but he's got to wear this S&M-looking brace for, well, this show and the next. Monica's got something to cheer him up though. She figures she needs a big engrossing project to take her mind off Richard, so she's decided to make real, from-scratch, jam. Joey, who loves jam deeply and profoundly, gets so excited that he downs a mouthful of the boiling hot brew while it's cooking on the stove. "This'll just be my batch," he says sheepishly after he spits it back in the pot. Joey, who was obviously in a heavy regression mode anyway, is transmitted back to around age six by the jam. He can't stop eating it; he takes it everywhere he goes. He has no shame. His face is constantly covered with the stuff.

In the meantime, a preppy looking "J. Crew guy" has been following Phoebe all over town for days. He's a stalker all right, but an inept one, since he intended to be stalking Phoebe's twin sister Ursula. "I just want you to know that before I met

Call her crazy, but Phoebe thinks her stalker (guest star David Arquette) is really cute.

"Now, just as she's about to drift off, you hug her, then you *roll* her over to her side of the bed – *she* still thinks you're just hugging – and you slip away. Hug for her. Roll for you."

– Ross –

your sister," he tells Phoebe, "I used to be a regular guy who sold beepers and cellular phones." Phoebe tells him that he's not the first. Softy that she is, she asks him if he wants to get a cup of coffee. He gratefully accepts. She even lets him walk next to her.

That afternoon, Ross and Rachel find themselves in the rare position of being alone in the apartment. That is, until Chandler barges in. He needs counseling on couple-dom from an official couple. First he wants to know how to field that perennial female query: "Do I look fat?" He then moves on to bed etiquette. "Janice likes to cuddle at night which I'm all for," he explains, "but when you want to go to sleep you want some space. But how do I do that without, you know, accidentally calling her fat or something?" "We wouldn't know about that," Rachel answers smugly, "because we're cuddly sleepers." But after she leaves for work, Ross clues Chandler in on the sleeping thing, deftly demonstrating his own special hug-and-roll maneuver that moves a Significant Sleeping Other to the opposite side of the bed. Chandler is impressed.

The next day Phoebe informs the gang that this guy Malcolm isn't really a kook, but rather this real romantic guy. (And cute). And he just got a teensy bit carried away, that's all. Chandler isn't buying it. "Wake up and smell the Restraining Order," he says. Ross agrees: "Face it, you've got a crush on your sister's stalker."

Monica presents Joey with the last jar of jam and announces that she's got a new project now … babies. Chandler advises her that she'll definitely need bigger jars. Ross asks if she hasn't forgotten something – like a dad. "I don't need an actual man," Monica replies. "Just a couple of his best swimmers and there are places where you can go to get those things now." The gang tries to be supportive, or anyway, as supportive as they can be given that they are totally creeped out by this idea.

In the meantime, when Chandler tries Ross's move on Janice he ends up flipping her off the bed. The next day at Central Perk, Janice happens to mention to Rachel that crazy Chandler spun her off the bed trying to do Ross's hug-and-roll thing. Rachel is not amused. Nor is Ross who lets Chandler in on one more couple constant: women talk.

Monica now has the info on the candidates from the sperm bank. But wait a minute, here's one describing a certain 27-year-old Italian American, an actor, born in Queens, from a family of seven sisters who sounds very familiar. "Joey, this is you!" she shrieks. "Yeah, it is," he answers casually. No big deal. However, he is surprised to hear that "there are any of my boys left." Monica tells him the competition is pretty heavy. "Maybe I should call them and tell them about my *Days of Our Lives* gig," Joey muses. "Juice that puppy up a bit."

The guys are still concerned that Phoebe is hanging out with the stalker. Joey suggests that she follow him and see where he goes to find out if he's really reformed. She tracks him into the 14th Street subway station but she's very bad at this game and immediately gets caught. She feels badly until Ursula strolls by. "Is that why you're here – because you know she uses this station?" That's why he's there, all right. Even though he's seriously contrite, Phoebe says she obviously can't date him anymore because he's like, you know, insane.

The next day as Monica is leaving for the sperm bank Joey asks her what the guy she picked is like. "Dark hair, green eyes," she answers. He says it's funny but he'd always imagined her with a blond guy, with a swimmer's body and a name like Hoyt. In fact, the picture of her and her husband and their children is so real to him he can actually see it. By the time he's through, even Monica can see it and suddenly she realizes what she'd be missing without a dad. And the sperm bank goes the way of homemade, from-scratch jam.

"Hey, it took me twenty-eight years to find one man I wanted to spend the rest of my life with. If I have to wait another twenty-eight, I'll be fifty-six before I have a baby. And that's just stupid."
– *Monica*

The Metaphorical Tunnel

Director:
Steve Zuckerman

Writer:
Alexa Junge

Chandler overcomes his fear of commitment, only to have Janice get cold feet; Phoebe becomes Joey's new agent; and Ross is worried when baby Ben falls for Barbie instead of GI Joe.

"Either you're seeing someone behind my back, or you're pretending you're seeing someone behind my back which is so pathetic I could just start crying right here in the cereal aisle."

– Janice

CHANDLER IS VERY UPSET. LAST NIGHT HE AND JANICE went out to a restaurant and she gave him half her chicken piccata and then she took all of his tomatoes. And that's bad because … why? Ross asks. Isn't it obvious? Because the two of them are starting to act

Matthew Perry fools around during a break in filming and finds a novel place to stash his phone during a break.

REGARDING WHAT FREAKS CHANDLER OUT:

"This is based on the fact that whenever I eat dinner with my boyfriend he gives me his red onions without thinking. Everybody felt that red onions were too weird a food for Janice to like, so it changed to tomatoes."

ALEXA JUNGE

like a couple. It's that old fear-of-commitment monster rearing its ugly head. The women know exactly what is going to come next; he'll get all mean and distant until she ends up breaking up with *him*. Joey is amazed. You *know* about that? They certainly do. All too well. But then Chandler

stops himself. He's really crazy about Janice. What is he running from? This time he's going to get through that tunnel ... you know, that tunnel with commitment on the other side.

The next night Chandler gives Janice a special present ... contact paper. "What do you say when the person you're sleeping with gives you contact paper," she says. But there's more. It goes with her own drawer. That's right, Chandler is giving her a drawer in his chest, in his apartment, in his life and – Oh MY GOD – she knows what a big step this is for Chandler. It was his fear of commitment that helped to break them before. But this time around, she's the one who's got commitment anxiety. After all, she's not even divorced yet. She doesn't know if she's ready for all this. She grabs her things and rushes out. Chandler hurriedly leaves her a message on her answer machine to apologize for what he's about to do – which is chase her down the street.

Joey's career is really in a rut. Lately, he's been reduced to doing infomercials touting a pouring spout. When Phoebe makes a call for him as his agent, she's so good that Joey wants her to do it full time. The problem is Phoebe hates getting negative feedback about Joey – like that he's "pretty but dumb" and "not convincing as a human." But Joey assures her that rejection is part of the acting game. But Phoebe's candor eventually convinces him that he should go back to his old agent. It's either that or blow

"Chandler, we said be aloof, not a doof."

– Monica –

his pretty dumb brains out.

Monica and Rachel try to help Chandler get through this current crisis with Janice. They tell him that he shouldn't seem too needy. Instead of calling, he just should run into her accidentally on purpose. So he begins to haunt the grocery where Janice shops. "What are you doing here?" Janice asks in amazement. Shopping, of course, Chandler replies. But he doesn't live in this neighborhood. Yeah, well, he's going to a party. Where? In Chelsea. Whose party? Chelsea's. Janice says, "Either you're seeing someone behind my back – which would make you the biggest jerk on the planet – or you're pretending you're seeing someone which is so pathetic I could just start crying right here in the cereal aisle."

Later when Chandler describes this exchange to Monica and Rachel, it's so painful they can barely listen. But then the phone rings and it's Janice and everything's okay. That would never happen with a man, Rachel and Monica observe disgustedly.

And Ross? Well, he can't say exactly why, but he's deeply uncomfortable watching baby Ben playing with his new Barbie. Susan and Carol swear that it was totally Ben's choice. Ross tries everything he can to get Ben into GI Joe and monster trucks, but Ben just isn't interested. Ultimately, Ross has no choice but to chill after Monica reminds him that when he was little he used to dress up as a woman named Bea.

THE ONE WITH
Frank Jr.

Director: **Steve Zuckerman**
Writers: **Shana Goldberg-Meehan & Scott Silveri**

Phoebe hopes to do some serious bonding with her new-found half-brother Frank Jr., and everyone makes a list of the five celebrities they'd most like to do it with.

JOEY IS OUT OF WORK, FOR A change, so he figures he'll make good use of his time by building a TV cabinet for the apartment. Admittedly, his carpentering skills are a little rusty – which might be why he makes the cabinet twice as big as it should be. Joey, however, is sure his ruler is wrong.

Chandler tells the guys about his Freebie List – a list of five different celebrities he's allowed to sleep with and Janice can't get mad. He's got Kim Basinger, Cindy Crawford, Halle Berry, Yasmine Bleeth, and Jessica Rabbit. Monica says first she needs a boyfriend then she'll get a list. Rachel reels off her choices very fast: Chris O'Donnell, John F. Kennedy, Jr., Daniel Day Lewis, Sting, and Parker Stevenson. But Ross has to give this some serious thought. He'll have to get back to them.

> ## "Sound the bell and gather every man you can – we've got ourselves an entertainment unit raising."
>
> *– Chandler –*

The next day Ross is back with his partial list of Elizabeth Hurley, Susan Sarandon and Isabella Rossellini. Chandler stops him. Isabella Rossellini is too international. She's never around. "Oh, cause *that's* why he won't get Isabella Rossellini – cause of geography," Rachel snorts.

Phoebe is really excited because her new-found half-brother, Frank Jr., is coming in from upstate New York for the weekend to do some serious bonding. Frank Jr. is pretty excited too. The first thing he wants is to go down to 42nd Street to buy some ninja stars and then take a picture of a hooker. But mostly, what the two of them do is sit together in silence. Finally, Phoebe asks him about his interests. He says he likes to melt things. Phoebe spends the rest of evening watching him melt a

spoon until the fumes give her a headache and she goes to bed.

Ross has finally completed his official list – which is so official he's had it laminated. Rachel reads: Uma Thurman, Wynona Ryder, Elizabeth Hurley, Michele Pfeiffer, and … *Dorothy Hamill*? "You *do* know she only spins like that on the ice?" she asks him.

The next day (small world) Isabella Rossellini herself walks into Central Perk. Wouldn't you know it? Just after Ross took her off his list. "Why, 'cause otherwise you'd go for it," Monica laughs. Yes, he would. And he will. Right now. Rachel sits back to watch the show. As he tells the beautiful actress about The Freebie List, she starts to laugh. "Don't laugh," he says. "This is a once in a lifetime opportunity." "Yeah, for *you*," she says – pegging the situation correctly.

By Phoebe's second day with Frank Jr. she's almost relieved when she gets a call to come in to work. "What do you do?" Frank Jr. asks her. She's a masseuse, she tells him. "At a massage parlor?" he asks incredulously. "We don't call it that," Phoebe says, "but yeah." She asks if he would like to come with her and get a massage. "Really?" he says,

totally boggled. His erroneous take on the situation gets him in hot water with his masseuse, Jasmine. "Wait, what's the deal?" Frank Jr. says. "You mean I can have sex with you but I can't touch you?" Phoebe is livid. "*That's* what you thought I did?" she yells at him. "This is the perfect ending to a perfect weekend," she says – not meaning it at all. It *was* perfect, Frank Jr. says sincerely. He tells her what a great time he's had and how he can really talk to her because she's his sister. By the time he finishes, Phoebe has totally forgiven him. "You know what my favorite part of the weekend is?" she asks him. "Right now."

"You mean I can have sex with you but I can't touch you?"
– Frank Jr.

Producers David Crane, Marta Kauffman and Kevin S. Bright with special guest star Isabella Rossellini.

The Flashback

Director:
Peter Bonerz
Writers:
**Marta Kauffman
& David Crane**

The gang is sitting around at Central Perk one night, when Janice asks who in the group has slept together. The answer is none. Okay then, she says, how about "almost?" Now that's a different story.

Eric asks Chandler if he would have a problem with models running in and out of the apartment if he moved in.

THREE YEARS EARLIER ...

MONICA'S NEAT FREAK FIXATION HAS DRIVEN HER roommate Phoebe to move in with her grandmother – and everyone knows, but Monica. Phoebe finally comes clean after Monica sees her sneaking stuff out. "I need to live in a land where people can spill," she tells Monica. She loves her, she says, but if she stays, she won't for much longer.

Monica is afraid that her quirks make her unlovable. "Is this why I don't have a boyfriend?" she asks her buddy Chandler from across the hall. Chandler tells her she's one of his favorite people and one of the most beautiful people he's ever known in real life. They hug and for a moment it seems like things might go further. But they end up saying goodnight as the good friends they are.

That night, Monica goes out to the bar downstairs with Chandler and runs into Rachel, a girl she'd known in high school. Rachel is there with two

of her girlfriends celebrating her engagement to a dentist named Barry. Rachel tells Monica with a profound lack of enthusiasm, that they must have lunch the next time she's in the city. Back at her table, she tells her girlfriends that what she really needs is one last fling before she gets married. Meaningless sex with the next guy she sees. Chandler overhears her and pops his pool ball in her direction. Naturally, Rachel freezes him out. But driving home, she has a torrid fantasy about that crazy guy in the bar.

Ross tells Phoebe he's finally figured out why his wife Carol has been acting so distant lately. She needed a friend and now she's found one at the gym named Susan, and he's sure things are going to change now.

Chandler is interviewing guys who've answered his ad for a roommate. He hates them all until he meets a photographer named Eric. There might be a problem though, Eric warns him: he's a photographer and that means there will be lots of models

Rachel tells her friends that what she needs is meaningless sex with the next guy she sees.

coming in and out. Chandler thinks he can handle that. They've got a deal. All Chandler has to do to wind up this hellish process is get one last guy out of the way. He's an Italian guy in a leather vest with greasy hair, named Joey Tribbiani.

Monica and Phoebe's downstairs neighbor, Mr. Heckles, knocks on the door to complain about the noise. As he turns to leave, he sees Eric about to go into the apartment across the hall and asks him what he's doing. Eric tells him that he's Chandler's new roommate. He can't be, Mr. Heckles informs him, because he is. Goodbye, Eric.

Hello, dense Italian guy.

Monica invites Joey over to her place for lemonade and tells him to make himself comfortable. Gotcha, he says excitedly and proceeds to rip off his clothes. "Cover yourself up," she orders him, as she beholds him completely starkers. "I can't believe this," she says in a state of shock, "Someone asks you in for lemonade and that means they want to have sex?" He's sorry, he says sheepishly, he thought she liked him.

Ross was right. Things do change between him and Carol – particularly after she tells him she's a lesbian. Phoebe comforts him as they sit alone together in the neighborhood bar, and then they suddenly find themselves in a passionate clinch. Ross throws her down on the pool table, hitting his head on the lamp. He tries to get on the table with her, but he can't get the pool balls to go into the pockets. Realizing this isn't going to work, they instead start to laugh. And it's a good thing, because Monica, Chandler and Joey come in just then. Seeing that Ross is upset, Monica asks him what's wrong. My wife's a lesbian, he says with a catch in his voice. Joey says, "Cool." Oh, by the way, Chandler says, Ross this is Joey. Joey, Ross.

"For me, the hardest part of 'The One With The Flashback' was trying to get Phoebe to the point where she would believably kiss Ross. They're so much like brother and sister that it almost seemed incestuous."

DAVID CRANE

Marta Kauffman, David Crane and director Peter Bonerz give notes to Mathew Perry and Courteney Cox as first assistant director Ben Weiss looks on.

Matt LeBlanc

"I thought, 'Oh great. This is a really good-looking guy. And he's going to be a total dick.' But he turned out to be a total sweetheart."

David Schwimmer

When Joey needs a particular credit on his résumé, he just makes one up.

NEXT TO COURTENEY COX, THE PERSON WHO MOST intimidated the other actors in the cast was Matt LeBlanc. All they really knew about him was that he had done one of those artsy-fartsy Levi's 501 commercials and that he looked a little too good.

Apparently they thought he was going to be one of those annoying Calvin-Klein-model types. "I thought, 'Oh great, here's this guy I'm going to be working with for maybe five years, and he's fucking Joe Cool stud," David Schwimmer recalls of his first meeting with LeBlanc. Jennifer Aniston was likewise afraid LeBlanc would be ultra macho. "I was scared of that type of guy," says Aniston, "which he thinks is very funny now."

Matt LeBlanc is anything but the pretentious brooder. On the contrary, as Joey the aspiring actor and adorable himbo, Matt LeBlanc has been extremely good natured about playing dumb and dumber. (Producer Kevin Bright's favorite Joey moment occurs when Chandler pays Joey $5 to climb into the grotesquely oversized TV cabinet he's built for their apartment. "Hel-lo Mr. Lincoln!" Joey hoots delightedly, oblivious to the fact that Chandler has locked him in.) As Joey, LeBlanc can make "What?" seem funny. And the chemistry between him and Matthew Perry gets better with each new season. When they start up with each other – Joey with his deadpan implacability and Chandler all seething frustration – it's almost as if they are Laurel and Hardy reborn as '90s urbanites.

Joey Tribbiani is something of a Neanderthal when it comes to male-female relations. Like, for instance, he hit on Rachel while she was still in her wedding dress. And the first time he was alone with Monica he got completely naked when she told him to make himself comfortable. Joey assumes that every woman he meets wants him. He wants them too – for the night. As Lisa Kudrow has observed, "Joey is every girl's nightmare – very sweet, but you know he's eventually going to cheat."

For three years now, the women on *Friends* have been doing their best to pull Joey into the '90s. And sometimes he actually seems to be making progress. In one episode he actually spends the whole night talking to a woman rather than doing the Other Thing. He's never going to become a Sensitive Guy, of course, but at least he'll be able fake it a little better.

The actor who manages to make all this blatant narcissism funny, and sometimes even endearing, is Matt LeBlanc. Matt was born on 25 July, 1967 in the working-class town of Newton, Massachusetts. He is the only child of an Italian-immigrant mother,

MATT LeBLANC

TELEVISION

TOP OF THE HEAP - Series Regular - FOX - Prod: Ron Leavitt
VINNIE & BOBBY - Series Regular - FOX - Prod: Ron Leavitt
T.V. 101 - Series Regular - CBS - Prod: Scott Brazil
ANYTHING TO SURVIVE - MOW - ABC - Prod: Edgar Scherick
CLASS OF '96 - Guest Star - FOX - Dir: Bethany Rooney
RED SHOE DIARIES - Guest Star - Showtime - Dir: Ted Kotchoff
JUST THE TEN OF US - Guest Star - ABC - Dir: Jonathan Wiess

TRAINING

Julie Ariola - Scene Study/Workshop
Flo Salant Greenberg - Private and Workshop

SKILLS

EXPERT MOTORCYCLE RIDER, SKYDIVING, BOXING, MASTER CARPENTER

(3/11/94)

**A total dick ... with that face?
And even if he were, who cares?**

Like Joey, Matt LeBlanc is into the carpenter thing.

who raised him in a small apartment while holding down a job as a production supervisor at a electronics company. "It was just me and my mom when I was growing up," says the self-professed Mama's Boy. "We're still very tight."

As a teenager LeBlanc was "considered a gearhead" because he went to a technical vocational high school and majored in carpentry. Although he learned his craft well enough to one day earn a living, he was mostly interested in partying and messing around with motorcycles and cars. In other words, he was an all-American boy. At eighteen he left

> "Matt's an unbelievably nice guy in the body of a tough, get-out-of-my-way guy."
> MATTHEW PERRY

Newton to live with his father in Florida. He then moved to New York – where he convinced two flight attendants to let him share their apartment by telling them that he had a trust fund when, in fact, all he had was a $3,000 stash from selling his truck. In New York, he eventually stumbled into modeling. Although he worked regularly, he didn't exactly make it big. At five-feet, eleven-inches he was considered too short to get the really high-paying gigs. "Modeling is all about the clothes anyway. I didn't want to stand still all day having my picture taken just to show off a jacket." In the interim he made ends meet by working nights at the hamburger joint Fatburger.

Eventually, Matt got into acting by doing television commercials for Levi's, Coke, Heinz ketchup, and Doritos, among others. He also began auditioning for parts in off-Broadway plays – which is where, as he says, he "fell in love with the craft of acting." In

Sometimes Monica has no choice but to knock some sense into Joey.

1988, he enrolled in formal acting classes. Within a year, he had landed a starring role in the television series *TV 101* and moved to Los Angeles. That short-lived series was followed by two more flops – *Top of the Heap* and *Vinnie & Bobby*. The fact that he won starring roles in so many series in so short a time was a clear indication that he had something. Still, if not for *Friends*, his career might have stumbled along like Joey Tribbiani's. (Although, really, what actor has taken the knocks Joey has? He's been Pacino's butt double and one of his reviews said he had "achieved new levels of sucking.")

Of all the Friends, Matt LeBlanc may be the most down-to-earth. He still plays with his cars and motor-cycles and even races on occasion. (Though that pastime may be on hold following a recent smash-up at a celebrity grand prix where he ran into a wall trying to cut off Jason Priestley.) Mostly though, he hangs with his dog Lady (a mutt he bought for $40 at the pound) and pals he's had for many years. "I have friends from all different walks of life, which I really like," he says. "If you put all of my friends together in one room, it would be very funny."

By the way Matt, the guy you used to work for at Fatburger wants you to call him. He's lost your number and you're not listed.

> "I'm not a dumb guy.
> I just play one on TV."
>
> MATT LeBLANC

Costume designer Debra McGuire created a kind of greaser look for Joey.

Costume design by Debra McGuire

The Race Car Bed

Director:
Gail Mancuso

Writer:
Seth Kurland

Ross tries to bond with Rachel's cranky father; Joey teaches a class in soap-opera acting; and Janice betrays Chandler with the Mattress King.

Phoebe explains to Monica why she signed for the race car bed.

THE GANG IS SITTING AROUND WATCHING THE TUBE when Janice's soon-to-be-Ex, the Mattress King, pops up doing a commercial. There is no happiness in the King's domain tonight, he laments, and so, he's having a sale. Janice can't believe his using their break-up to sell beds. Monica too is appalled. Still, look at those prices. She's got to go check the sale out. But Chandler must never know. Monica goes to the store the very next day and finds a heavenly bed at a royal price.

Joey is teaching a class in soap-opera acting at the Learning Connection. One of the most important things in soap-opera acting, he tells his students, is re-acting. Oh, and before he forgets ... "to work in soap operas," he tells them, "some of you are going to have to become much more attractive."

On a roll, Joey also has an audition for *All My Children* as a boxer. As he and Phoebe do a little practice bobbing and weaving, she punches him in the nose and gives him a nosebleed. While Phoebe's busy attending to Joey's nose, the Mattress King's delivery guys carry a child's race car bed into Monica's bedroom.

Back in class, Joey shows his students a few tricks of the trade. Like, if he has to cry, he just cuts a hole in his pants pocket and tweezes a hair from down there. Afterwards one of his students tells him he's got an audition and asks if he'll coach him. What's it for? Joey asks excitedly. *All My Children*, his student replies, for the role of Nick the boxer. A few days later, Joey watches his student perform the audition scene. The guy's great. Joey's totally impressed. "Tweezers?" he asks. No, the guy says … just him. "Any suggestions?" the student wants to know. Joey tells him to play the boxer gay.

"It's just that the guy is so good," Joey guiltily confesses to the gang later. "Oh, then it's okay," Phoebe says not at all sincerely.

By the next class it looks like Joey has learned his lesson. And he has in a way. "I advised a fellow actor to play a role homosexually,' he tells them, his voice cracking with emotion. "We both auditioned for the part and as it turns out, they liked the stupid gay thing and they went with him. And now he has a two-year contract with Susan Lucci. And I'm stuck here teaching a bunch of people who are too ugly to be on TV."

Rachel wants Ross to go to dinner with her and her father. "But he hates me," Ross protests. "He calls me Wet Head." She promises that she'll wear that black thing he likes if he'll come. At dinner, Dr. Green asks how things are going at the library. Ross says he supposes they're fine, but he works at the museum. When Dr. Green goes over to say hello to some friends, Ross notices that he only tipped a measly 4%. "You're a waitress. Doesn't that bother you?" he asks Rachel. As they're leaving Ross quickly throws down a twenty. But Dr. Green finds it and demands, "Do you think I'm cheap? I pay two hundred for dinner and you put down a twenty and you look like a big shot. Okay Mr. Big Shot, *you* pay the bill."

Rachel insists that Ross try again with her father. "You've got to be the bigger man." She's already got a mother and father who can't be in the same room, she tells him. She can't stand it if she's going to have to have a separate room for him too.

Dr. Green comes over for brunch the next Sunday and starts immediately with the Wet Head routine. However, the two men end up bonding by dumping on Rachel for her many shortcomings.

Meanwhile, Joey goes with Monica to the Mattress King's store to insist he take the race car bed back. But as he storms into the office, he sees Janice kissing her Ex, the King himself.

Careful there, guys. The Mattress King's delivery-men hoist producer Kevin Bright on the set of "The One With The Race Car Bed."

The Giant Poking Device

Director:
Gail Mancuso

Writer:
Adam Chase

Baby Ben gets a bump on his head while playing airplane with Monica; Phoebe thinks she's killed Ugly Naked Guy by going to the dentist; and Chandler tells Janice to go (not go).

ROSS GETS AN EMERGENCY CALL FROM THE MUSEUM. Some children have defaced the *Homo sapiens* exhibit by painting over the word "*sapiens*" and rearranging the figures in a very naughty way. He asks Monica if she'll look after Ben while he attends to the matter. "But what about me?" Rachel pouts. Ross explains that he, uh, only asked Monica because she has no life. But, of course, she should watch Ben too.

But later while they're all playing the airplane game, Monica throws Ben up in the air and he bangs his head. Hard. Rachel is furious. "How could you *do* that?" she screams. "Ross trusted me." Monica suggests that they not tell him. But what about that bump on Ben's head, Rachel wants to know. How do they not tell him about *that*?

Ross sees the bump right away, but he's not the least bit angry with Rachel. Kids bump into things all the time," he tells her, just the slightest bit overbearingly, "You have to watch them all the time." "I did!' she protests. "I watched Monica bump his head into that thing!"

Chandler is going to get Janice something extra special for her birthday. Joey suggests bubble gum or, better yet, a barium enema. He's not too keen on Janice since he saw her kissing her Ex (on last week's show). "Oh God, here's the thing," Joey finally breaks down and tells him, "I went down to the Mattress King's Showroom and I saw Janice kissing her ex-husband."

Chandler confronts Janice with her duplicity and she becomes so agitated it looks like she's going to faint, or throw up, or something. Chandler gives her a paper bag to put over her mouth. The truth, she nods frantically, is that she loves both him and her Ex. Chandler is devastated. Not just about Janice, but about the now-totally-useless 12-pack of condoms he bought that morning. Later, Joey tells him that if it were him, he would bow out. After all, Janice is a married woman with a child. "If there's a chance, they can make it work," he says, "I know I wouldn't want to be the guy who stood in the way of that."

"Well, they painted over the word *sapiens*, for one thing. Then they ... rearranged the figures. Let's just leave it at that."

— *Ross*

Ugly Naked Guy is alive, but he is *not* happy.

Phoebe has a terrible toothache but she hates going to the dentist because every time she does, someone dies. That's why she takes such good care of her teeth now: she flosses to save lives. At the gang's urging, Phoebe finally goes to the dentist. Afterwards she is relieved to hear that no one is dead. There is someone who isn't looking so hot though. Joey has noticed that Ugly Naked Guy hasn't moved since early this morning. Phoebe is sure she killed him. Joey suggests that they make an extra long pole from their old chopsticks to poke him. "What we're about to have here," Phoebe wails, "is a naked dead man on a stick!" They steer the pole out the window and toward the body. Ugly Naked Guy moves! He's alive. However, he is definitely *not* happy. And he shows them *his* poking device to prove it.

In the meantime, Chandler tells Janice that he just can't be responsible for breaking up a family. He remembers how he felt as a kid whenever he saw the guy who came between his parents. It didn't matter how happy he made his father. Janice knows he's right, but she has one last thing to tell him: "What we have," she says, "it's like movie love. You're my soul mate. And I can't believe we're not going to be spending the rest of our lives together." Upon hearing this, Chandler caves immediately. "Then pick me!" he yells. He steals one of her shoes to keep her from leaving. But it's too late. She hobbles away. Forever?

Janice tells Chandler that now she knows what Lionel Richie has been singing about all these years.

"In terms of life imitating art, a number of things have happened to me that have directly paralleled what's happening with Phoebe and it really freaks me out. Like her whole dental thing — suddenly I had to have a root canal the same week! There's some strange connection that Phoebe and I have."

MARTA KAUFFMAN

The Football

Director: **Kevin S. Bright**
Writer: **Ira Ungerleider**

Ancient rivalries are re-ignited as the gang plays a friendly game of touch football.

IT'S THANKSGIVING, THAT WARMEST OF HOLIDAYS, and the gang is in a football mood. They don't just want to watch it; they want to play it. Or anyway, a few of them do. Chandler is still torching for Janice. "Come on," Joey says, "you never want to do anything." Do so, Chandler says: "I want to wear my bathrobe and eat peanut clusters all day." Monica and Ross would like to but their mother won't let them. It seems that when they were playing touch football during the Sixth Annual Geller Bowl many years ago, Monica broke Ross's nose – or as he puts it, "When she saw I was going to tag her, she threw her big fat grandma arm in my face." While their dad rushed Ross to the hospital, their mom threw the much-coveted Geller trophy into the lake.

By the time they've finished recounting this saga, Monica and Ross are ready to relive the Geller Bowl all over again. They all head for an empty lot and choose up sides with Monica and Ross as the team captains. Monica picks Joey. "But Monica, I'm

your best friend," Rachel whines. "Don't worry, Honey, you'll get picked," Ross says, and then proceeds to choose Chandler. Monica taps Phoebe. "See, Sweetie, I told you you'd get picked," Ross tells Rachel. But, as she points out, there's no one left.

The action is dominated by Monica's team and they move ahead quickly with Joey carrying the ball. Even Phoebe makes a touchdown – although Ross insists that the buzzer sounded. As for Rachel,

Ross tells her to "go long" so many times, that she finally goes long for a pretzel. Monica and Ross bicker through every play and he continually accuses her of cheating. "Why don't you just admit it," she jeers. "I'm better than you." Then she gets a little cocky. "Tell you what, I'll trade you Joey for Rachel," she challenges, "and I'll still win."

A very slick-looking Dutch girl in a mini and spikes asks Chandler and Joey if they mind if she watches. As they walk back to the game, Joey magnanimously offers to let Chandler have her. "You'll *let* me have her! Chandler snarls. "Whadaya mean, like, if you didn't, I wouldn't have a shot?" Right, Joey shrugs. Chandler is going to have to teach Joey a lesson. First he tears his favorite jersey. Then he asks, "Oh by the way, Joey, where do Dutch people come from?" Joey is pretty sure he knows the answer: "Well, uh, the Pennsylvania Dutch come from Pennsylvania." "Enough with the geography for the insane," Ross breaks in. "All right, Heidi," he asks her, "which one of my boys do you like?" Well, if she has to choose right now, she says, she would have to say Chandler. "I win. You suck. I rule all." Chandler chants as he dances around Joey. "Mini-wave in celebration of me." Miss Holland suddenly decides that she's not interested in Chandler either. She now finds him shallow, and how you say, a "dork."

Ross goads the guys: we are losing to *girls*! On the other side of the field, Monica likewise exhorts her team to win this game for women everywhere! To even up the odds a little, Phoebe flashes Chandler whenever he gets the ball. Then Rachel jumps Joey and rides him across the field with Phoebe and Monica holding her legs. Positive they're going to lose anyway, Monica throws the ball to Rachel; Rachel goes long like she's been doing the whole game, but this time she catches the ball in the endzone for a touchdown! The girls go wild. But by Chandler's quick calculations, she was five feet short. Doesn't that mean the ball is still in play, Phoebe wonders, as Monica and Ross dive for the ground.

Later that night while the rest of the group sits down to their turkey, Monica and Ross are still sprawled on top of the ball as it slowly starts to snow.

"How come it's always us left on the field holding the ball?"

– Ross –

(Above) **"C,mon guys," Ross exhorts Joey and Chandler, "we're losing to *girls*."** (Left) **Joey tells Margha that he's pretty sure Dutch people come from Pennsylvania.**

Rachel Quits

Director:

Terry Hughes

Writers:

**Michael Curtis &
Gregory Malins**

It's Christmas time and Rachel has no job and no prospects; Phoebe wants to save dried out Christmas trees from a fate worse than death; and Ross breaks the leg of an eight-year-old Brown Bird.

GUNTHER TELLS RACHEL THAT her boss wants her to take her waitress training over again. She's shocked, she tells Chandler, as she lounges with him on the sofa. But as Gunther patiently puts her through her paces the next day, she realizes that she's training to do a job she hates. Joey and Chandler urge her to be brave and quit: "If you quit this job, you then have the motivation to go after a job you want," Joey says. "I would give anything to work for a designer or a buyer," she admits. "I don't want to be 30 and still work here." "Yeah," says Chandler, "that would be much worse than being 28 and working here." All right, she'll do it. Chandler leans over to Joey and asks him if this means they're going to have to start paying for coffee.

> **"If you ask me, so long as you've got this job, you've got nothing pushing you to get another one. You need 'The Fear.'"**
>
> *– Joey –*

Ross breaks a Brown Bird's leg demonstrating his backswing to Chandler in the hallway and he feels terrible. The little girl turns out to be an eight-year-old named Sarah whose life sounds like it came straight out of the *Times*' "Neediest Cases." She helps her father clean apartments, she tells Ross – that is, when he's not playing the slots in Atlantic City. But Sarah's a plucky sort who has dreams of becoming an astronaut. That's why she was going door-to-door the day Ross clobbered her: she was selling cookies to win a trip to Space Camp.

Like Ross wasn't already guilty enough.

Chandler prints up Rachel's anemic résumé – which he then proceeds to make fun of in front of Ross. Rachel thinks that's rich – seeing as he's the

one who talked her into quitting in the first place. But then, Joey bursts in to tell her that he can get her an interview at a place called Fortunata Fashions. But Rachel blows the interview big time. "I wouldn't have even hired me," she tells everyone afterwards. And now she can't even get her old job back because they've already hired someone else.

Ross decides *he'll* sell the cookies for Sarah. How hard can it be? No wait, maybe he'll just buy them all from her. How much are they, he asks as he gets out his wallet. Five dollars a piece, she says. So what's second prize, he asks as he puts his wallet away. It's a ten-speed bike but she'd rather have something her dad can't sell. So Ross sets out to do the door-to-door cookie-selling thing. But when people see him, they assume he's an ax murderer.

Joey has a part-time job selling Christmas trees, but Phoebe feels sad for all those innocent trees that are cut down in their prime. Joey assures her that they're fulfilling their life purpose by making people happy. But when Phoebe goes to visit Joey on the lot, she's horrified to see the old dried-out trees get ground into pulp. She screams so loudly you'd have thought they were putting her grandmother in the wood chipper. Phoebe then tries to talk all of Joey's customers into buying the old codgers.

Ross ends up pawning off a bunch of cookies on the gang – especially Monica who has a longtime Brown Bird cookie addiction. "I ate every one of my boxes and Dad bought them all, remember?" she

asks Ross. "No," Ross corrects her. "Dad had to buy all of your boxes *because* you ate them." In the end, Ross ends up selling 517 boxes mostly to students at the NYU dorms where he's known as Cookie Dude. Sadly for Sarah, Ross ends up losing to a girl who gave her uniform to her nineteen-year-old sister who sold them to sailors at the SS Nimitz.

There are happy holiday endings all around as Rachel gets the job at Fortunata Fashions after all; Ross and the guys create their own silly space camp for Sarah, and Monica and Joey rescue all the old homeless Christmas trees and buy them as a present for Phoebe.

Matt LeBlanc and Lisa Kudrow with David Crane and his father Gene Crane, a Philadelphia news anchor.

Friends ...

MONICA

MONICA

Pete Becker (millionaire)
– Jon Favreau –
(TOW The Hypnosis Tape)

Dr. Richard Burke (older guy)
– Tom Selleck –
(TOW Monica And Richard Are Friends)
•
Mischa (translator)
double date with Phoebe
– Stephen Kearney –
(TOW Ross And Rachel Take A Break)
•
Julio (bus boy/poet)
– Carlos Gomez –
(TOW All The Jealousy)
•
Fun Bobby (alcoholic)
– Vincent Ventresca –
(TOW Russ)
•

Jean-Claude Van Damme
– himself –
(TO After The Superbowl)

RACHEL

RACHEL

Ross
– David Schwimmer –
•

Mark (co-worker/the other guy)
– Steven Echoldt –
(TOW All The Jealousy)
•

Tommy (the screamer)
– Ben Stiller –
(TOW The Screamer)
Barry (ex-fiancé/left at the altar)
– Mitchell Witfield –
(TOW Barry And Mindy's Wedding)
•
Paolo (Italian Stallion)
– Cosimo Fusco –
(TOW Ross's New Girlfriend)
•
Michael (blind date)
– Arle Gross –
(TOW Ross Finds Out)
•
Russ (a Ross-a-like)
– Snarro (aka David Schwimmer) –
(TOW Russ)
•
Jean-Claude Van Damme
– himself –
(TO After The Superbowl)

PHOEBE

PHOEBE

Vince (fireman)
– Matt Battaglia –
(TOW Ross's Thing)
•
Jason (teacher)
– Robert Gant –
(TOW Ross's Thing)
•
Robert (hanging brain guy)
– Marcus Flanagan –
(TOW Monica And Richard Are Friends)
•
Sergei (diplomat)
– Jim Pirri –
(TOW Ross And Rachel Take A Break)
•
Malcolm (the stalker)
– David Arquette –
(TOW The Jam)
•

Rob (the library guy)
– Chris Isaak –
(TO After The Superbowl)
•
Ryan (sailor)
– Charlie Sheen –
(TOW The Chicken Pox)

Duncan Lipper (ex-husband)
– Steve Zahn –
(TOW Phoebe's Ex-Husband)

# of Friends

JOEY

Kate (actress)
– Dina Meyer –
(TOW The Screamer)
·

Lauren (understudy)
– Jennifer Milmore –
(TOW The Screamer)
·

Ginger (one-legged girl)
– Sherilyn Fenn –
(TOW Phoebe's Ex-Partner)
·

Erika (the stalker)
– Brooke Shields –
(TO After The Superbowl)

CHANDLER

Janice
– Maggie Wheeler –
(TOW The Princess Leia Fantasy)
·

Joanna (Rachel's boss)
– Alison LaPlaca –
(TOW The Dollhouse)
·

Mary Angela (Joey's sister)
(TOW Chandler Can't Remember)
·

Margha (girl at football game)
– Susanna Voltaire –
(TOW The Football)

Jude (wrong number girl)
– Brittney Powell –
(TOW 5 Steaks And An Eggplant)
·

Susie (underpants girl)
– Julia Roberts –
(TO After The Superbowl)
·

Ginger (one-legged girl)
– Sherilyn Fenn –
(TOW Phoebe's Ex-Partner)

ROSS

Rachel
– Jennifer Aniston –
·

Julie (the new girlfriend)
– Lauren Tom –
(TOW Ross's New Girlfriend)
·

Carol (the ex-wife)
– Jane Sibbett –
(TOW The Ski Trip)

Chloe (Xerox girl)
– Angela Featherstone –
(TOW Ross And Rachel Take A Break)
·

Caitlin (first date after Rachel)
– Laura Cayouette –
(TOW The Screamer)
·

Bonnie (the bald girl)
– Christine Taylor –
(TO At The Beach)

Chandler Can't Remember

Director:
Terry Hughes

Writer:
Alexa Junge

Chandler tries to remember which of Joey's sisters he groped at Joey's birthday party, and Rachel gets her dream job at Bloomingdales with the help of a dreamy admirer.

CHANDLER GETS HAMMERED ON Jello shots at Joey's birthday party and fools around with one of Joey's sisters in a storage room. The problem is he can't remember which one. And there are *seven* of them. And they all look alike. And they all could take Chandler with one armed tied behind them. (If Joey didn't get to him first.)

The morning after the party, Joey gets a call from his sister Mary Angela telling him what happened. He slams into Rachel and Monica's – where Chandler is hiding – and demands to know if he's interested in his sister or is just using her to get over Janice. "Gotta be the first one," Chandler stammers.

"Don't think I haven't noticed your potential," Rachel's boss tells her as she makes him coffee for

"Jell-O just like Mom used to make."

– Chandler –

the umpteenth time. But he's got a new job for her that's a lot more related to fashion – separating hangers! At the diner later, Rachel complains to Monica, "How much am I going to learn about fashion by walking Myra, the arthritic seamstress, to the bathroom?" A really cute guy at the end of the counter chuckles softly at her story. "Is my misery funny to you?" she says. But the guy explains that he was only laughing because he had to sort mannequin heads at Mannequins Plus when he was first starting out. By the way, he adds, there's an opening in his department at Bloomingdales and would she be interested? Rachel offers him her pickle.

Chandler tries writing a letter of apology to Mary Angela, but Ross tells him this is something that's got to be done in person. "You just go to the house and ask for Mary Angela." "And if she doesn't answer the door?" Chandler inquires.

But when Chandler knocks on the door of the Tribbiani house, it's Joey who answers. Chandler tells him that he's, uh, come to see Mary Angela. Joey says great and invites him for dinner. Surrounded by the sisters at a big table, Chandler asks, "Who this, Mary Angela?" and "What's that, Mary Angela?" But Joey's grandmother answers every question, and Chandler almost belts her. Suddenly the sister next to him tells him to meet her in the bathroom. She's all over him as he begins to apologize. But she's not listening. "Mary Angela was right," she tells him, "you *do* have the softest lips." Chandler shrieks, "If *you're* not Mary Angela, then who is?" At that moment Mary Angela appears behind him and says darkly, "I am." Then she screams, JOOOEEY, at the top of her lungs. Joey comes racing in and she orders him to punch out this clod. Ordinarily Joey would be happy to punch

anyone, but this is Chandler. He figures he ought to at least give him a chance to explain. "If you wanna punch me go ahead, I deserve it," Chandler begins to apologize yet again, "But I would never soberly hurt you." The sisters still want Joey to mangle him and one of them even offers to do it herself. But Joey vetoes that, on the condition that Chandler tell Mary Angela he's sorry. When Chandler still doesn't know who Mary Angela is, Joey says, "Okay, Cookie, *now* you can punch him."

Rachel excitedly tells Ross about the job interview at Bloomingdales this really nice guy named Mark Something got her. "This guy is helping you for no apparent reason?" Ross asks her in disbelief. "Sounds like Mark Something wants to have some sex." But Ross doesn't have anything to worry about. Or does he?

Ross is waiting for Rachel after her interview when Mark rushes out of the elevator to tell her she got the job. She's so excited that she hugs him – Mark, that is.

Don't mess with them. The Tribbiani sisters and their Nana.

CHANDLER

You guys can't tell them apart

either! Hah!

PHOEBE

We didn't make out with one of

them. Hah! Hah!

~~CHANDLER~~

CHANDLER

Wait! I know. Veronica! In the   *

green dress. I definitely stuck my

tongue down her throat.

MONICA   *

Uh, that was me.   *

CHANDLER

(HANGS HIS HEAD) Sometimes when

I've been drinking, I can become a

little overly friendly. Sorry.

RACHEL/MONICA/PHOEBE/ROSS

That's okay.

RACHEL   *

You didn't sleep with Joey's

sister, did you?

CHANDLER

No! (THEN, EMBARASSED) Though in

some countries I'd have to marry

Mr. Treeger's old bean bag chair.

JOEY ENTERS. AD LIB HELLOS. HE GOES TO CHANDLER.

JOEY

I need to talk to you.

DOES IRA KNOW THIS is ABOUT HIM?

NOW I DO! Thanks, LEX!

WAS THIS Scott's JOKe?

did STANdards Sign off ON THIS?

SUCKERS

— 120 —

All The Jealousy

Ross acts like the jealous fool he is when he thinks Mark is after Rachel; Joey blows a job in a Broadway musical; and Monica gets poetic justice after being dissed by a Latin lover.

Director:
Robby Benson
Writer:
Doty Abrams

RACHEL IS STARTING WORK AT BLOOMINGDALES AND she is seriously nervous, but fortunately she has Mark – who got her the job – to show her the ropes. Ross, who's sure Mark is after Rachel, showers her with little tokens of his love – including an original song written by Ross and performed in her office by a real live barbershop quartet. Rachel is embarrassed until Mark explains that Ross is just marking his territory. Or as Rachel complains to Ross later, "You might as well have just come in and peed all around my desk."

Joey is up for a new job too – a singing part in a musical version of *A Tale of Two Cities*. It turns out that the part also requires him to dance. "With your background," the assistant director assures him, "it'll be a piece of cake." He seems to think Joey has danced with Twyla Tharp and the American Ballet Theater. But maybe that's because he's put that on his résumé.

"Can you, like, dance at all?" Phoebe asks him after hearing about his predicament. Sure, he says, and then he does his best cabbage patch. At the call-back the next day, the assistant director tells Joey to take over for him and teach the group some flashy moves he quickly demonstrates. But Joey teaches the dancers the only thing he knows. "That's the best I could get out of 'em," Joey tells the director, as the group does the cabbage patch.

Meanwhile, Monica has eyes for Julio, the humpy waiter who works with her at the Moondance Diner. She's impressed with how smart he is and that he's a poet. He's impressed with her too – particularly her lower lip, as he demonstrates.

Joey tells Ross how sad, how impossibly pathetic his life is going to be if he doesn't get this jealousy thing under control.

> ## "You don't do anything.
> ## Play it cool. Just keep it inside.
> ## Learn how to hide your
> ## feelings. Don't cry out loud!"
>
> *– Chandler –*
>
> *advising Ross on how to handle his jealousy*

The next day Monica rushes in to Chandler and Joey's to show them a poem Julio wrote while they were fooling around last night. She's totally dense about this stuff, she says, and she wants to know what they think. It's called "The Empty Vase". They all

Julio has written a special poem about Monica called "The Empty Vase".

say it's great, but after she leaves Phoebe says she feels really bad. The guys don't get it. Don't you see, she says, the poem was about a beautiful vessel with nothing inside. He wrote that about *Monica*. Later, she gently tells Monica her interpretation of Julio's poem.

Ross decides to make a surprise visit to Rachel's office. But as he hesitates outside, Mark draws his own girlfriend – who also works there – into an embrace. "I can't help it," he tells her, "I'm just so crazy about you." Rachel coos, "Oh, that's so sweet." Of course, all Ross can hear is Mark and Rachel. He bursts into the office yelling, "All right, that's it. Get off of her!"

Chandler has the happy (for him) job of booking a stripper for a bachelor party for his weird cousin Albert. He decides to go with a certain Crystal Chandelier – who apparently has some very special talents involving grapes. At Central Perk a few days later he proudly shows Rachel the nudie pen he got as a party souvenir. When Ross stops by he apologizes to Rachel for his jealous outburst and she eventually lets him off the hook. "Where are you going?" she asks as he gets up to leave. "To a play date with a woman I met at the party," he answers. "Wait a minute, you met a woman at the bachelor party? The stripper? You have a play date with a stripper?" she says in disbelief. It turns out that she's got a boy Ben's age. Rachel suddenly feels it necessary to send Ross off with a scorchingly hot kiss. "That should hold him," she smugly tells Chandler. "Either that or you just turned him on and sent him off to a stripper," Chandler replies.

Back at the Moondance Diner, Julio is coming on to yet another woman when the barbershop quartet suddenly rushes in and performs another original ditty – this one by Monica who turns out to be something of a poet herself.

MONICA'S ODE TO JULIO

Mr. Pretentious,
You think there's no one finer,
Well your poems are all un-published,
And you work in a diner.
You think you're God's gift to women,
But that's all in your head.
You are just a butt-munch.
(No one likes a butt-munch)
And you're also bad in be-e-ed.

Music by Michael Skloff.
Lyrics by Doty Abrams and Daniel Ferris.

Monica And Richard Are Friends

Monica and Richard run into each other; Rachel and Joey discuss literature; and Phoebe dates a guy who keeps coming out of his shorts.

Director:
Robby Benson
Writer:
Michael Borkow

(Left) **"Are you sure you only want to be friends?"** Richard asks Monica on his cell-phone.
(Below) **It's tough work but somebody's gotta do it. Producer Marta Kauffman romances Tom Selleck during a rehearsal break.**

PHOEBE IS DATING A GUY FROM CALIFORNIA NAMED Robert who's really great with the exception of one thing: he's always coming out of his shorts – or as Chandler puts it, "The man is showing brain!" Ross suggests that they try not to look directly at it … like an eclipse.

Monica and Richard run into each other in a video store after being apart for six months. He tells her she looks great (even though she's got panties stuck to her sweats, which she just took out of the dryer). They start talking and one thing leads to another and pretty soon they're spending more and more time together as "platonic" friends. But one day he calls her and asks her if she's sure she wants it to stay that way. "We're being smart," she assures him. And she even thinks she means it, till she discovers that he's calling from outside her door. The next time we see them they're lying together in bed and Monica is musing, "We can be friends who sleep together." He agrees, "It's something we do like racquetball." Just out of curiosity, she wonders, does he have any other racquetball buddies? He tells her

he has a blind date with his sister's neighbor next Tuesday, but he'll cancel it if it would make her feel better. But she says she wouldn't want him to do that, because after all they're just friends.

Rachel wonders what a copy of *The Shining* is doing in Joey's freezer. He tells her that he got scared

reading it and put it there. He feels safer that way. It turns out that it's his favorite book: he's read it over and over. That's the way Rachel has read *Little Women*, she tells him, but that's different. It's a classic. Joey says *The Shining* is a classic too. They agree to trade books and report back. There's just one thing that Joey wants to know: these little women … how little *are* they? Are they like scary little?

Meanwhile, Monica has had a rotten day at the diner that ended with her fake boob catching fire. As she heads into her room, Rachel observes slyly that there's still a chance for her day to pick up. Monica heads into her room and there waiting for her, amidst dozens of roses, is Richard holding two glasses of wine.

A few days later, Monica sets out to surprise Richard by doing the rose-and-wine thing for him,

but as she waits in his bedroom, she hears him come into his apartment with a date. The woman says she wants to see his place. He shows her around, but then he opens the door to his bedroom and sees Monica hiding under the covers on his bed. That's it, he tells the woman and now he's *really* tired so goodnight. After she's gone, Monica asks who she was. His blind date, he says – the one he told her about. Do you like her? she asks. And hey, she's fine with it if he does. No she's not. Not at all. "What if we're friends who don't see other people?" she proposes. No wait, "What if we're friends who live together, or friends who vow to be friends forever in front of their friends?" He tells her they're back where they started and of course, she knows he's right. She says she's got to get out of there right now because getting over him is the hardest thing she's ever had to do. Before she goes though, she wonders if he'd like one last game of racquetball?

Back at Central Perk, the guys refuse to say anything to Robert about his ventilation problem. No, they'd rather fall on the floor laughing and make stupid jokes about him. It looks like Phoebe is going to have to do the dirty work herself until Gunther happens to get a panoramic view of Robert's shortcoming and tells him, "Hey buddy, this is a family place, put the mouse back in the house."

Amazingly, Joey really gets into *Little Women* – although it takes him a while to figure out who's a girl and who's not. By the end, he's so upset when Beth dies, that Rachel has to put the book in the freezer for him.

> "He taught me how to do all sorts of jock stuff. I learned how to shoot a layup, a foul shot, and a twenty-three-pointer."
> – *Phoebe*

> "Robert's coming out of his shorts."
> – *Chandler*

THE ONE WITH
Phoebe's Ex-Partner

A new girl folksinger at Central Perk turns out to be Phoebe's old partner; Chandler confronts his true feelings about artificial legs; and Ross is jealous of Rachel's passion for her new career.

Director:
Robby Benson
Writer:
Wil Calhoun

Don't trust her, Phoebe. Jingle Bitch will sell you out.

THE GUYS ARE IMPRESSED BY LESLIE, A GIRL SINGER who's recently started playing at Central Perk. Phoebe says she's okay if you like a song with lines that rhyme. But Phoebe has more against Leslie than her rhymes and the fact that she can play guitar and sing at the same time. The two of them used to be singing partners, until Leslie abandoned her to go Big Time.

Chandler and Ginger get cute at the men's room at Central Perk and they start dating. But then Chandler finds out that Ginger has had a thing with Joey and it did NOT end well. In fact, Joey says, what he did to Ginger is the most awful, horrible thing he's ever done in his whole life. It seems the two of them went up to her dad's cabin for a romantic weekend. After dinner, they fell asleep in front of the fire. When Joey awoke and saw that the fire was dying out, he picked up a log and threw it in the fireplace. But that log was Ginger's artificial leg. So he did what anyone would do. He ran.

The whole leg thing freaks Chandler out too. "I like her," he tells Monica. "I don't want to stop seeing her. But every now and then, it's like – hey, where's your leg?" But then one night as Ginger and Chandler are about to get intimate, she gets a gander at his third nipple and she's so repulsed she ends up running away from *him*.

Leslie really wants to get back together with Phoebe again. But Phoebe freezes her out not once but twice. "Let that be a lesson to you," she warns the gang afterwards. "Once you betray me, I become like the Ice Woman. Nothing can penetrate this icy exterior." Later Phoebe tells Monica the whole story. She and Leslie go way back to when they were kids

(Top right) **Chandler's freaked out by Ginger's wooden leg. But just wait till she finds out about his third nipple.**

> "Sticky shoes! Sticky shoes!
> Always make me smile!
> Sticky shoes! Sticky shoes!
> Next time I'll avoid the pile!"
>
> Music by Michael Skloff and Lisa Kudrow.
> Lyrics by Wil Calhoun.

together. The two of them were a team, but then Leslie dumped her to work for a jingle house. Phoebe says she can't take the chance of letting her back in her life. Still, those years they played together were the most fun she's had in all her lives.

A few nights later when Leslie is singing the Phoebe classic, "Sticky Shoes Always Make Me Smile", Phoebe can't resist and starts singing with her. Friends again, Phoebe sings "Smelly Cat" to Leslie and she is blown away. Up to her old tricks again, Leslie

takes "Smelly Cat" to the people at her old agency anyway and they love it. Phoebe tells Leslie to choose – "Smelly Cat" or her. Leslie chooses the money. But Phoebe's okay. Sort of. She's got a great new song called "Jingle Bitch Screwed Me Over."

Meanwhile, Rachel and Mark are going to a fashion lecture together. Why, Ross wants to know. Because he's her friend, that's why. "Do you really need another friend?" he asks sincerely. She wants a friend who has the same interests she has, she tells him. None of you guys would want to go to something like that. Would too, he says. But at the lecture, Ross wants to cuddle. Then he embarrasses her by falling asleep and snoring. He defends himself by saying the lecture was boring. Rachel says his bone stuff at the museum is boring too. "Oh yeah?" he retorts, "A hundred million people went to see a movie about what *I* do. I wonder how many would go see a movie called *Jurassic Parka*. A bunch of outta-control jackets take over an island." "Then why did you go with me?" she wonders quite reasonably. He knows it's dumb but he hates not being a part of her new life. She says, "My work is for me. It's scary, but I love it 'cause it's mine."

"Oh, God, it freaked me out! I mean, I know it shouldn't have, but it did! I like her a lot. And I don't want to stop seeing her. But it's like – hey – where's your leg?"

– *Chandler* –

THE ONE WITH PHOEBE'S EX-PARTNER

                    JOEY

I wish. (THEN) After dinner, me,
Ginger, and Pepper, all fell asleep
in front of the fire. I woke up in
the middle of the night and saw the
fire dying out. So, I picked up a
log and threw it on. Or... at
least what I thought was a log.

                    PHOEBE

DO YOU THINK
WE'RE GOING TO
GET FLACK FROM
HANDICAPPED GROUPS
WITH THIS?

Oh, my god. You threw Pepper into
the fire.

                    JOEY

I wish. (THEN) See, I guess
another thing I should've told you
about Ginger is that she kinda has
an artificial leg.

                    PHOEBE/MONICA

Oh, my god. Oh, my god!

                    PHOEBE

You threw it in the fire??

                    MONICA

She must've totally freaked out.

                    JOEY

(BEAT) Yeah, she must've.

                    PHOEBE

You don't know?

                    JOEY

Well... uh...

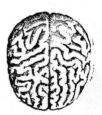

Bright
Kauffman
Crane

> drive carpool
> ride horse
> talk to Kevin re:
    cut
> Camera blocking
    9:30 AM
> check wardrobe
    (Courtney)
> make list for
    soccer snacks
> talk to David
    re: outline
> talk to Nancy
    re: deals
> Back to school
    night ???
> reservations w/ Michael

MARTA KAUFFMAN

Ross And Rachel Take A Break

Director:
James Burrows

Writer:
Michael Borkow

Joey and Chandler fantasize about a kinky night with Chloe, the girl in the Xerox place, but it's Ross who nails her after Rachel suggests they "take a break."

CHANDLER AND JOEY ARE CRAZY FOR CHLOE, THE sexy girl in the Xerox place with the bellybutton ring. When she makes a little joke about the three of them doing something together, it makes Joey snicker and scares Chandler to death. Later, it occurs to the guys that maybe they should establish some ground rules, just in case Chloe wasn't kidding. Joey says his first would be: never open your eyes – "because you don't want to be doing what you're doing and then look up and see something you don't want to see." But then Chandler points out that if you're not looking, you might touch something you don't want to touch – a yucky thought that makes them both twitch. Joey then wonders where each of them would be in that kind of situation. But he guesses they could just flip a coin. Still, which end would be heads, and which would be tails? Chandler says, "If you don't know *that*, we shouldn't do this."

Phoebe has a new love interest too – a dashing diplomat she met while giving free massages at the UN. (She figures bodies at peace make peace.) The only problem is that Sergei doesn't speak English and his translator keeps getting in the way, especially during romantic moments. Phoebe talks Monica into coming out with them to dinner, but Monica and the translator get along so well, Phoebe and Sergei can only stare into space.

On an equally discordant note, it's Ross and Rachel's anniversary, but a crisis keeps her at work until very late. But Ross, sweetheart that he is, surprises her with a picnic dinner complete with candles and wine. The problem is that he – and his lovely little gesture – are really in the way, particularly after he sets her desk on fire trying to light the candles. "Got to call you back," Rachel growls into the phone, "I've got Shemp in my office." After more unfriendly words, Rachel sends Ross home.

Later at the apartment, Rachel expects an apology but instead Ross forgives *her*. Okay, she'll try again. "You do *not* bring a picnic basket to a person's work," she berates him. "Unless maybe they're a park ranger." It's just that he's beginning to feel like he doesn't have a girlfriend any more, he tells her. What's the big deal? It's just a job. Now she's really going to have to kill him. "Ross, do you realize that

"You don't bring a picnic basket to a person's work! Unless maybe I was a park ranger!"

– Rachel –

this is the first time in my life I'm actually doing something I *care* about?" she asks him. But Ross still doesn't get it and, she's beginning to think he never will – especially when he asks her if this isn't really about Mark. "Maybe we should just take a break," she says softly. "Okay," he says, getting his coat, "let's get some frozen yogurt or something." "No," she tells him, "a break from *us*." He gets it now – and bolts out the door.

Meanwhile, over in a neighborhood bar, Chloe is entertaining Chandler and Joey with stories from the wonderful world of copying and collating when the heartbroken Ross shambles in. Chloe jumps up to greet him. She's crazy for this guy because of his unique reproduction needs. The two of them dance and Chloe asks him if he's married, not that it matters. They get closer and Ross gets drunker as the night wears on.

Knowing she's made a terrible mistake, Rachel sits by the phone. But it's Mark, not Ross, who calls and insists on coming over. And it's Mark's voice Ross hears in the background when he finally does call Rachel later. He slams down the phone, his worst suspicions confirmed.

Rachel calls Ross's apartment over and over again, but Ross doesn't hear the phone because he has brought Chloe home.

(Left) **Sergei doesn't speak English and his translator keeps getting in the way.**

(Below) **Chloe grooves on Ross because he has kinky copying needs.**

> "I thought they were on a break and it was okay for Ross to sleep with the girl from the Xerox place, but I'm in a monogamous relationship."
>
> MICHAEL BORKOW
>
> "I thought they were on a break and that he truly believed that Rachel was in the midst of having an affair with Mark because he was there in her apartment after they'd just had this huge blowout. I mean, why else would he BE there?"
>
> ADAM CHASE
>
> "We get a lot of stories from this kind of argument. When you've got a show with six characters who are constantly talking-talking-talking, you've constantly got to come up with things for them to take sides on."
>
> DAVID CRANE

Matthew Perry

"Matty's one of the most sensitive people I've ever met, more than most girls I know."

Jennifer Aniston

COULD HE BE ANY MORE ADORABLE? OR ANY smarter or more likable? The answer is no and no again. So, are we talking about Chandler Bing or Matthew Perry? That would be a definite yes all around since, of all the *Friends*, Matthew Perry probably has the most in common with his small screen alter ego.

TV viewers often mistakenly make the assumption that their series favorites just make up their lines as they go along. But the one case where that exception is quite often the rule is Matthew Perry – who is every bit the incorrigible wise-ass as his character. Initially the *Friends* producers didn't anticipate that many storylines would revolve around Chandler. But that was before they and the writers got to know Perry. The more time they spent with him, the more his idiosyncratic speech cadences began to crop up in Chandler's dialogue.

Chandler waxes serious on the subject of his third nipple to Phoebe and Joey.

Soon, Perry's own life began to seep into the show's storylines. After listening to him describe a date from hell along with his worries about ending up alone, for example, the writers wove the incident into a Chandler story arc. "I'm not dead," Chandler would soon moan after a disastrous romantic encounter, "and yet I have no life." Over the last few seasons, many of Perry's suggestions for jokes and plot turns have found their way into the show and he is the only Friend who has been allowed to sit in on the writers' sessions.

All this creative give-and-take is a welcome change for Perry, who considers himself to be as much a writer as an actor. On his earlier sitcom outings, Perry had felt stifled creatively. "I have been in certain TV shows and movies where I was just a talking head – just read the line the way it's written and go home." But he had more to offer than that. "I thought, 'Hey, I can be funny in this kind of format and situation. Please let me.' But most of the producers I have worked with didn't. Which is why it was such a relief to get to the set of *Friends* where they said, 'If you come up with some funny things and we think they're funny, we'll put them in.'"

"I was convinced I could write something better than the things I had been in on television," Perry says of the period in the early '90s when he began writing scripts. Not only did he co-write a sitcom pilot which caught the eye of NBC, but he has co-written a movie called *Imagining Emily* about a man who falls in love with a grown-up version of his imaginary childhood friend – in which he is scheduled to star some time next year. By the way, his sitcom was called *Maxwell House* and it was about a group of friends who sat around a New York coffeehouse talking about their lives. By all accounts the script was pretty sharp. The problem was that NBC already had something remarkably like it in the works.

Born on 19 August 1969, in Williamstown, Massachusetts, Perry is the son of actor John Perry – familiar in the 1960s as the face of Old Spice cologne – and Suzanne Perry, then a model. Like Chandler, Perry's parents' marriage was cut short by divorce. Before his first birthday, he and his mother moved to her native Ottawa, the city he still considers home. His mother began working in several different capa-cities within Canada's federal Liberal party. She and young Matthew moved around a lot

The boy's got it all (including "TOW Five Steaks And An Eggplant" guest star Brittney Powell).

during this period, but they ultimately settled again in Ottawa in 1978 when she became a press aide to Pierre Trudeau. "My recollection of that time mostly was, 'Wow, she's working a lot, and I wish she wasn't,'" Perry recalls. As for school, Perry says, "I was a horrible student." He spent much of the day at Ottawa's exclusive Ashbury College just goofing around – and honing the unusual verbal tic he shares with Chandler, a way of emphasizing certain words for sarcastic effect.

Perry's mother remembers him as being a more determined than comical child. "He's very, very, very serious," she says. From an early age, her son

had a clear set of priorities – and school was not among them. "He used to say to me, 'Why do I have to go to school? I will *never* use this. I want to play tennis and I want to act.'"

Perry spent his childhood on the tennis court. "When everybody else was hanging out, I was going down to the tennis club, which was frequented primarily by 60-year-old men, and hoping that one of them wouldn't show up, and I could be the fourth in a doubles match." By the time he was 13, Perry was the No. 2 player in Ottawa. In doubles, he and his partner placed third at the Canadian National Championships in his age group. Because his goal was to play professional tennis, he decided to move to Los Angeles to live with his father, who had moved there to act. "It was an opportunity for me to get to know him," he says. Happily for his

Chandler is casually hip when not on the job as a computer programmer.

Costume design by Debra McGuire

Hey, you woulda hired him too ...

They're the Laurel and Hardy of the small screen ... Matt LeBlanc and Matthew Perry.

mother, who missed him terribly, she moved to L.A. herself two years later. Perry continued to play tennis until he lost a big match in front of his whole family. It didn't help that he had begun to vent his frustration on the court in the manner of his idol, Jimmy Connors. "Nine times out of ten, I'd win, but I'd still be upset," he recalls. "So I completely stopped playing after graduation."

Perry's tennis ambitions were quickly left in the dust after he was "discovered" by director William Richert at the age of 15. He was skipping classes from the tenth grade and sitting in a restaurant with three girls. "I was trying to be funny in an effort to impress them. And I got a note on a napkin from Richert saying he would really like me to be in his next movie and to call him. So I did and two months later I was on the set of *A Night in the Life of Jimmy Reardon* in Chicago [opposite River Phoenix]. This would be a much better story if the movie had been a huge success." Even though it wasn't a hit, Matthew Perry had an acting career from that day forward, and even though you probably didn't really notice him until he became Chandler Bing, he's been working steadily for over ten years. He starred in four failed series and did dozens of guest star roles as well as another film, *She's Out of Control*, during that time. More recently, he has starred in *Fools Rush In* and the upcoming *Edwards and Hunt* with Chris Farley. Although notoriously insecure and tough on himself, Perry acknowledges that whatever happens in his big screen career, he has a heckuva day job to fall back on. He might even know now that the thing his millions of fans love most about Chandler Bing is watching Matthew Perry play himself.

MATTHEW PERRY

MOTION PICTURES
PARALLEL LIVES - Showtime Films - Linda Yellen, dir.
SHE'S OUT OF CONTROL - WEG/Columbia - Stan Dragoti, dir.
A NIGHT IN THE LIFE OF JIMMY REARDON - Fox - Wm. Richert, dir.

TELEVISION
LAX 2194 - Universal/FBC - Pilot
DEADLY RELATIONS - Wilshire Court Prod./ABC - MOW
HOMEFREE - Universal/ABC - Series Regular
BEVERLY HILLS 90210 - FBC - Guest Star
WHO'S THE BOSS - ABC - Guest Star
CALL ME ANNA - Gilbert Cates Prod./CBS - MOW
SYDNEY - Columbia/CBS - Series Regular
EMPTY NEST - NBC - Guest Star
GROWING PAINS - ABC - Recurring
JUST THE TEN OF US - ABC - Guest Star
HIGHWAY TO HEAVEN - NBC - Guest Star
DANCE 'TIL DAWN - Konigsberg-Sanitsky/NBC - MOW
CHARLES IN CHARGE - Syndicated - Guest Star
BOYS WILL BE BOYS - FBC - Series Regular
TRACEY ULLMAN SHOW - FBC - Guest Star
MORNING MAGGIE - CBS - Pilot
SILVER SPOONS - Syndicated - Guest Star

The Morning After . . .

Director:
James Burrows

Writers:
**Marta Kauffman
& David Crane**

Rachel finds out that Ross had a close encounter with Chloe, the girl from the Xerox place, and breaks up with him – this time, for real.

Ross thought they were on a break.

IT'S THE MORNING AFTER RACHEL'S BUST-UP WITH Ross. She's barely slept from agonizing over the way she left things with him last night. Ross, on the other hand, has just awakened to find that he's apparently had an intimate encounter with Chloe, the babe from the Xerox place. He's pretty sure he has since she just came out to say good morning to him dressed only in a towel. He stumbles out of bed to play his answer phone messages and is overjoyed to hear Rachel saying that she loves him and that she'll stop by on her way to work in the morning to tell him so in person. Ross looks at his clock in horror: she's due ... *now*. Just then Chloe ambles out of the bedroom looking for her shoes. She wants to get friendly again, but he hurriedly piles her things in her arms and flings opens the door to nudge her out. But there standing in the doorway is Rachel – just about to knock. He pushes Chloe behind the door as he envelops Rachel in a hug.

Ross manages to get Rachel out before she realizes that Chloe is there, but later he tells Joey and Chandler that he's got to tell her the truth about what happened. "How dumb *are* you?" Chandler wants to know. "If you have to tell her, at least wait till the timing is right. That's what deathbeds are for." To their relief, Ross eventually agrees that the truth will only hurt her. Joey says that now he's got to make sure she doesn't find out any other way and did Ross cover The Trail? What trail? Chandler tracks it for him: Chloe to Isaac, the guy she works with at the Xerox place; Isaac to his sister Jasmine, who works at the massage place with Phoebe; Phoebe to ... Obviously, Ross had better get busy.

Ross starts with Isaac, but he's already told Jasmine. Jasmine thinks Ross did a bad, bad thing, but she agrees not to tell Phoebe. However, she tells him he should probably talk to her roommate Gunther since he knows Phoebe too. Ross rushes in to the coffeehouse, but it's too late: Gunther has already told Rachel. (No surprise: Gunther has been torching for Rachel for one whole season, at least.)

While Ross and Rachel's romance is falling apart, Monica and Phoebe are busy giving themselves a leg wax with some fancy organic junk Monica ordered from TV. It's supposed to be painless, but as they rip it off they start to scream. They're so loud that Chandler and Joey come rushing in to Monica's bedroom to save them from some terrible fate. Shortly afterward, Ross and Rachel come in and immediately start arguing. The four of them rush to the door to eavesdrop on what's happening. But then they end up getting stuck in the bedroom as Ross and Rachel go at it for hours.

Ross tells Rachel that when he slept with Chloe, he thought their relationship was dead. "Well, you sure had a hell of a good time at the wake," Rachel retorts and then asks, "Say I had slept with Mark, would you still want to be with me?" Ross tells her that he would. From inside the bedroom, Monica, Phoebe, Chandler and Joey let out a collective sigh.

"I did a terrible, stupid thing," he tries again. "I wish I could take it back, but I can't." Rachel remains unmoved. She tells him that he's a totally different person to her now. And what they had is changed forever.

The two of them fall into an exhausted sleep and Chandler, Joey, and Phoebe finally creep out of the bedroom – casting sad looks in the direction of the sleeping couple as they tiptoe past them and out the door.

> "I'm sort of a combination of Ross and Chandler. Ross in that there's a part of me that's a solid, feet-on-the-ground guy. And Chandler in particular because of the way he uses comedy as a defense mechanism – as a way of staying safe and sane."
>
> DAVID CRANE

> "I can't believe this. This is the most horrible thing that's ever happened ever. I knew something had to be wrong. My fingernails did not grow at all yesterday."
> – *Phoebe*

"The One The Morning After" 23.
FINAL DRAFT Yellow Rev. - 12/20/96 (ALTERNATE #1) (II/P)

PHOEBE

(TO JOEY) What're they talking about?

JOEY SHRUGS.

ARE WE GONNA KEEP THEM IN MONICA'S ROOM FOR THE REST OF THE EPISODE?

CUT BACK TO:

YES

REALLY? ISN'T THAT A LITTLE STATIC?

NO

INT. LIVING ROOM - SAME TIME

RACHEL IS PACING AND WRINGING HER HANDS.

ROSS

Rachel, I --

RACHEL

No! Get away from me!

ROSS

It was a mistake. I made a mistake.

RACHEL

A mistake?! What were you trying to put your penis in, her purse?

we'll never get this past S&P.

CUT BACK TO:

INT. MONICA'S BEDROOM - SAME TIME *

PHOEBE

(INTRIGUED) What was he trying to put in her purse?

CUT BACK TO:

INT. LIVING ROOM - SAME TIME

RACHEL

Ross, you had sex with another woman!

The Ski Trip

Director: **Sam Simon**
Writers: **Shana Goldberg-Meehan & Scott Silveri**

The rift between Ross and Rachel threatens to break up the group when everyone but Ross goes away on a ski trip with Rachel.

THINGS HAVE GOTTEN SO BAD BETWEEN ROSS AND Rachel that they can't even be in the same room with each other. And now they're starting to vie for the group's affections. Rachel tries to lure them into her camp with tickets for a Calvin Klein lingerie show. But Ross has already booked them. They all feel terrible about having to say no to Rachel, especially Joey who hates like crazy to be missing models in their underwear. But Rachel says she understands that Ross asked them first. Within minutes, Rachel is back to up the ante. How about a trip to her sister's cabin for a weekend of skiing?

Ross doesn't take it well when they tell him they're going away with Rachel. "That's okay," he sniffs, "if you guys all have to go away on the first weekend I'm by myself." Phoebe volunteers to stay since the last time she went skiing she just ended up going round and round on the chair lift because she was afraid to jump off. But Joey reminds her that they'll need her to drive them in her grandmother's cab. Monica then offers to stay. After all Ross is *her* brother. "What, a pity stay?" Ross says indignantly. No thanks.

The rift makes Chandler so nervous that he starts smoking again. "Why would you start again after chewing all that quitting gum?" Phoebe demands. "This is just like my parents' divorce when I started smoking in the first place," Chandler says. "Weren't you *nine*?" Monica asks in disbelief. "I'm telling you something, you can't beat that first smoke after nap time," Chandler replies.

That Friday night, as they're driving on the interstate, Phoebe stops Chandler from smoking so he insists on stopping to go to the bathroom. Phoebe pulls up at a lonely rest stop and everyone hops out – except Rachel who makes it a policy never to pee in public restrooms: "They never have

any toilet paper in there, so my rule is 'No tissue, no tushy.'" But then she changes her mind and jumps out too, locking the keys in the cab. Now Chandler is really upset because his lighter is in there. Joey ends up getting Phoebe to give him the wire in her underwire bra, which he uses to jimmy the door lock. But as Phoebe tries to start up the car, she rea-lizes that they're now out of gas.

Phoebe calls the Auto Club, but she's not exactly sure where they are. She thinks it's Route 27 or 93 or 76 so maybe somebody could just check every rest stop on all those roads? Nope, they don't do that, Phoebe says after she hangs up. Monica suggests that they just call Ross, but Rachel's not having any of that. Phoebe calls him anyway and tracks him down at Carol's. "Oh *now* you want a favor," he says to Phoebe, "Well, I'm sorry you're in

> **"You can't beat that first smoke after nap time..."**
> – *Chandler*

trouble, but I'm a little busy with my *real* friends now." Carol gives him the keys to her car and pushes him out the door saying, "We both know you're going to do it, because you're not a creep."

"What's *he* doing here?" Rachel demands as Ross pulls up in the car a few hours later. "If I'm stepping on your toes in which case I can just mosey on," Ross says, "I've got plenty of people to help on the interstate." The two of them end up embroiled in the never-ending "We Were On A Break" debate. They finally stop after Chandler has what looks like a seizure. (Actually, he was doing his impression of Shelley Winters in *The Poseidon Adventure*.)

Taking the lead, Phoebe admonishes the warring couple to figure out a way to be around each other "or otherwise that's it for us hanging out together." Ross and Rachel reluctantly agree to be civil. The others climb back into the cab and head out to the cabin, leaving Ross behind. But now *his* car won't start.

"The One Without The Ski Trip"
FINAL DRAFT - 1/23/97

RACHEL

I think it's pretty clear who's

wrong here.

ROSS

Obviously not to Joey.

JOEY

(STILL FEIGNING OBLIVIOUSNESS)

What?

ALL OF THEM BUT CHANDLER BEGIN ARGUING AT ONCE. ROSS
AND RACHEL GO AFTER EACH OTHER. JOEY'S MAD AT MONICA
FOR OUTING HIM. MONICA IS TRYING TO DEFEND HERSELF.
PHOEBE IS ATTEMPTING TO REASON WITH EVERYONE. CHANDLER
IS DESPERATE TO STOP ALL OF THIS.

CHANDLER

Hey! Guess what I am...

HE HOPS AROUND, SMOKING AND GESTURING IN SOME
INCOMPREHENSIBLE WAY. THEY ALL LOOK AT HIM A BEAT,
THEN ALL RETURN TO FIGHTING. FINALLY, PHOEBE CAN'T
STAND IT.

PHOEBE

Hey, hey, hey!

ALL BUT CHANDLER LOOK AT HER.

PHOEBE (CONT'D)

I mean, look what you're doing to

Chandler!

THEY ALL LOOK, CHANDLER'S STILL AT IT. SEEING THEM ALL
STARING AT HIM, HE STOPS.

MONICA

(GUILTY) Not just to Chandler...

Chandler was originally conceived as a secondary character who didn't have his own stories. He was just going to be the guy with the quippy one-liners. But once you have Matthew Perry who can be very funny and vulnerable and romantic, there's no place you can't go. When he does the realer moments is when I adore him the most.

MARTA KAUFFMAN

WHAT SHOULD MATTHEW BE DOING HERE?

JUST LET HIM BE MATTHEW.

Does Chandler have to smoke here?

Don't worry, everybody gives him shit about it.

The Hypnosis Tape

Director:
Robby Benson
Writer:
Seth Kurland

Frank Jr. finds love with his Home Economics teacher; Monica is pursued by a cuddly millionaire, and Chandler becomes a very dainty non-smoker.

FRANK JR., PHOEBE'S VERY UNUSUAL HALF-BROTHER, rushes into Central Perk to tell her that he's in love and he's getting married. Phoebe thinks that's fantastic. Frank knew she'd be cool. He goes to get his fiancée, who's parking the truck. The gang wonders if Frank Jr. might not be a little young to be getting married. Phoebe points out that he is eighteen. Ross says that means it will be illegal for him to drink at his own bachelor party. "Or get a hooker," Joey adds with concern.

Frank Jr. returns with an adorable, though much older woman named Mrs. Knight. She was his teacher in Home-Ec, he explains. "He was my best student," she giggles. "She was my best teacher," Frank Jr. says tenderly. Then they kiss – which makes everyone twitch. "You're not like I pictured you at all," Mrs. Knight tells Phoebe. "Yeah, *I'm* a big surprise," Phoebe manages to stammer.

Meanwhile, at the Moondance Diner, a bearded guy (John Favreau) who's sitting at the counter happens to overhear Monica pleading with Rachel to fix her up with somebody. The guy says he'll take a date if she's giving them away. "You only want to date me cause of the big boobs and the blonde wig and 'cause I serve you food," she laughs. "If that were true," he tells her, "I'd be dating my Aunt Ruth." Then the guy does another really cute thing: he leaves Monica a check for $20,000 as a tip. Later Chandler tells her that this guy is Pete Becker, the guy who invented Moss 865, a famous computer program. But now Monica is really mad. This rich guy apparently thinks he can buy her. But Pete assures her that all he wants is one meal with her. So he takes her for pizza in Rome.

Rachel is sick of Chandler's smoking so she gives him a hypnosis tape that worked for a woman in her office. Ross mutters that "hypnosis is beyond crap." She reminds him that she watched him get hypnotized in Atlantic City. He did NOT get hypnotized, he says. "No, 'cause you always pull your pants down and play 'Wipe Out' on your butt-cheeks," she retorts.

Every night Chandler plays the hypnosis tape while he's sleeping. "You're a strong confident woman who does not need to smoke," the voice on the tape murmurs in his ear. Before long, Chandler has not only stopped smoking but he's turned into

Monica wants somebody, anybody, to fix her up with a new guy.

an amalgam of Chandler and Nancy Reagan – a smart-ass with lovely manners and impeccable taste.

Phoebe begs Ross and Joey to talk some sense into Frank Jr. And they try. But as he describes how much in love he is, they're so happy for him that they all end up in a group hug. By the time Phoebe returns, Joey has agreed to be Best Man at Frank Jr.'s wedding and Ross is the ring bearer.

Obviously, she's going to have to take care of this problem herself. She convinces Mrs. Knight to go away. Frank Jr. is devastated. Phoebe tells Frank Jr. that it's for the best. He says, "Right, if the best is unbelievable pain." He was finally happy for the first time in his life. And now it's gone, and he doesn't know why.

Phoebe brings Mrs. Knight over to explain why she left. "I was being selfish. Even though we want the same things right now, in the future we might not." She stops in the middle of her speech to look at Phoebe to make sure she's saying it right. "Even though we love each other as much as we do," she continues, "nonetheless, you're too young to know what you want." Phoebe is glad they see things her way. That is, she is until they fall into a passionate embrace.

The Larry King Interview

In mid-March of 1997, as *Friends* was nearing the end of its third season as one of the reigning top ten shows in America, the cast finally accepted a long-standing offer to appear on CNN's *Larry King Live*. But the interview as conducted by the self-proclaimed King of Talk turned out to be as bizarre as one of Phoebe's daydreams.

For the first part of the interview, Matthew Perry, Jennifer Aniston, David Schwimmer, Courteney Cox, Matt LeBlanc and Lisa Kudrow good-naturedly answered questions about their salaries and their relationships with one another. But the real entertainment ensued as Larry's mind started to wander. First he introduced a clip from the show featuring Matthew Perry's character, Chandler, whom he rechristened as "Charles." After the clip, David Schwimmer asked King just who "Charles" was, and he responded, "Let me tell you something. The teleprompter is far away on this set. And I'm getting older." Later, when addressing Schwimmer, King called him "Richard." After being corrected, King explained, "You know what? Just then you looked like a Richard." Schwimmer shot back, "I understand, Steve." Later in the show, he mispronounced Lisa Kudrow's name, and couldn't seem to take in the fact that Matt LeBlanc had injured his shoulder on the set ("You got hurt?"). Finally, when King asked each member about his or her favorite episode, Matthew Perry quipped, "The One Where Larry Does Research."

In all fairness, it should be noted that Larry had announced a few days earlier that he was in love again and contemplating marriage for the seventh time.

The Tiny T-Shirt

Director:
Terry Hughes

Writer:
Adam Chase

Pete is in love with Monica; Monica is still hung up on Richard; Joey's got the hots for Kate; Ross is still in love with Rachel; and Chandler's gay. (Just kidding.)

Rachel tells Ross "he's a petty, petty man."

RACHEL TELLS ROSS SHE WANTS TO SEE HIM. HE'S sure it's because she's come to the realization that life without him sucks. But she just wants to return his stuff – hats and CDs and other little odds-and-ends. She tells him that it's time they move on. If that's the way she feels, he says, it's fine with him. So, where's the rest, he demands – like his "Frankie Says RELAX" T-shirt? Rachel is livid. He knows she sleeps in that shirt. And besides, he hasn't worn it since he was 15. It doesn't even fit him anymore. Oh yeah? He rips off his shirt, pulls it on and storms out of the apartment carrying his sad box of memories and wearing the teeny, tiny T-shirt.

(Right) "So where are we going with this ... whatever it is we're doing?" Pete asks Monica.

Pete asks Monica if they're going anywhere with this ... whatever it is they're doing. She tells him that it's just that she's at a place in her life where she wants to focus on her. Okay, she finally admits, she's just not attracted to him. He tells her that she may

end up feeling differently. "You seem awfully confident for a guy I just told I wasn't attracted to," she smiles. "Stupidly charming, isn't it?" he replies.

Pete is such a regular guy that the gang almost can't believe that he's a zillionaire. And he's their age! "Why am I only attracted to guys where there's no future?" Monica wails. Pete is such a great guy and they have such a great time together. He has everything. And then too, he actually *has* everything. Is something wrong with her? Phoebe says definitely yes.

And Joey? Well, he has a deep hostility thing for Kate, an actress he's working with in an off-Broadway play. "Just because she went to Yale Drama School," he rants to Chandler, "she thinks she's the greatest actress since sliced bread." It's obvious that Joey has a crush on this uppity chick, Chandler tells him, noting that he's done nothing but talk about her for the last 48 hours.

Kate doesn't understand why her character is attracted to Joey's character, she complains to the director. Joey feels the same way – since it says right there in the script that she's a bitch. "No, it doesn't," she counters. "It does in mine," he says with a satisfied grin.

> "What Kevin does in the editing room is so astonishing ... it's really magic! We'll see a cut of the show and say oh god, this is terrible and he'll take it away and I don't know what kind of spells he passes over it, but it will come back and it's hilarious. He's brilliant in the editing room.
>
> MARTA KAUFFMAN and DAVID CRANE

But while they're rehearsing a love scene together, Kate goes into an extended swoon after Joey really plants one on her. Joey asks her out for coffee afterwards, but she leaves with the director – like always.

Ross sees Rachel leaving going out with Mark and spends the rest of the night glued to the peephole at Chandler's apartment. "If she kisses him goodnight I'm going to kill myself, I swear," he moans. But they don't kiss. They go into the apartment together.

Chandler has to jump Ross to keep him from breaking down her door. "Unless you're thinking of subletting my peephole," he tells him, "you are going to have to get used to the fact that the relationship is over!"

Across the hall, Mark leans over to kiss Rachel, but she says she would just be doing it to get back at Ross. He suggests they get back at Ross together right there on the couch. Then he says he guesses he'll just have to get back at Ross back home all by himself.

The next day Rachel returns home to find that Ross has returned a box of her stuff, and in it is the teeny, tiny "Frankie says RELAX" T-shirt.

Ross was right all along ... Mark *is* after Rachel.

Kate says she doesn't know why her character would be attracted to Joey's character. Yeah, sure she doesn't.

David Schwimmer

"David has the craziest fans. When he goes out, you'd think The Beatles had arrived."

Courteney Cox

HE IS THE FRIEND WHO FIRST MADE YOU LAUGH OUT loud, the one you felt you really knew. It was David Schwimmer's undeniable appeal that led critics to single him out as the show's first break-out star. Somewhere along the way, he also became a pin-up boy – although he would be the first to admit that he's an unlikely heart-throb. And yet, *Playgirl* voted Schwimmer one of 1995's ten Sexiest Men. And his admirers on the Net spend hours typing his praises and composing online paeans to his puppy dog eyes. One enthusiast even sent him her underwear.

No one could have anticipated the frenzy *Friends* would inspire, least of all Schwimmer himself. Sidestepping his contributions, he instead attributes the show's success to its ability to tap into a deep-seated longing for family – no matter how unorthodox the form. "I think for some people it's a fantasy to have this close a group of people, to have a family, really of – well, I guess it's an attractive group. They're loyal, fun and, in a way, cool. So many people have grown up products of divorce or less than ideal family situations. And to have this kind of solid support group is something everyone wants in their lives."

Schwimmer further believes that the show has tapped into an evolving perception of friendship. "In my parent's generation, people have only one or two close friends," he observes, "whereas I literally have twenty *really* close friends who are constantly calling, crashing, or hanging out at my house at any given time. Not that we set out to, but I guess you could say that my age group has sort of reinvented family on its own terms. And I can't think of another show that's shown it the way *Friends* has."

Unlike his cast mates, all of whom are children of divorce, Schwimmer is the product of a long and successful marriage. Both of his parents are high-powered Los Angeles attorneys. (His mom handled Roseanne's divorce case.) Despite being a fortunate son, Schwimmer remembers himself as being something of a misfit as a child. "My big sister, Ellie, was the good one," he says. "I was a rebellious kid, always in trouble. I was constantly getting suspended from school – that's what happens when you're the class clown."

But school wasn't nearly so funny once Schwimmer moved into the country club atmosphere of Beverly Hills High: "I was always bigger than my friends until high school. Suddenly everyone else shot up, and I didn't grow. I was short and pudgy, and it turned me into a less than confident loser." Schwimmer felt out of place in the school that was the inspiration for *Beverly Hills 90210*. "I never felt good enough or good-looking enough there," he says now. "I was chubby and a nerd." Still, it was in high school that the acting bug bit David after he played a part in *West Side Story* alongside one of his best buddies (still), *The Single Guy*'s Jonathan Silverman.

For a time, David considered studying law or medicine, but a summer course in theater at Chicago's Northwestern University sold him on acting. He attended Northwestern for four years, graduating in 1988 with a BS in speech/theater. Schwimmer then used his own savings to co-found The Lookingglass Theater Company in Chicago with a group of fellow graduates. "Every actor had to pay a membership fee," he says. "That's what kept us rolling – that and waiting tables." After returning to LA he landed only one job in six months so he returned to Chicago again to work in the theater. Two years later, he returned to LA and landed recurring roles on *LA Law*, *The Wonder Years* and *NYPD Blue*, on which he played the memorable vigilante 4B.

If the role of Ross seems custom fit for Schwimmer that's only because it quite literally was.

Marta Kauffman and David Crane, the show's creators, remembered him from a past audition and wrote Ross for the voice they couldn't get out of their heads. And in fact, Schwimmer was the only cast member offered his part without an audition. But while other cast members may have been sure they had signed on to a hit (or so they say now) David Schwimmer was less than convinced. "I figured *Friends* was just another temporary thing. I was sleeping on a futon in a friend's living room in Chicago only two months before I filmed the pilot."

Ultimately though, it was the heartbreaking vulnerability Schwimmer brought to Ross that brought the show's future direction most clearly into focus for the show's creators. That may be because he sees himself first and foremost as a character actor – even when he's playing a leading man. As a highly trained stage actor, Schwimmer is most interested in what can be conjured up in the process of working on a role. "We do our most interesting work on the rehearsal set," he observes of the *Friends* cast. "That's where we bring things to life that aren't necessarily there on paper. For me, it's a process of making a story ring true emotionally. The writers work at night, but during the day, the actors own the set. I sometimes get the feeling that people think we just lounge around the set all day, but nothing could be further from the truth. We're constantly working to help each other come up with the most original way of doing things. We rely on directors to point the cameras in the right direction, but we have to depend on our own instincts about our characters. We're the ones who have catalogued every move, every gesture, every bit of business that's occurred over the last three years and it's up to us to make sure everything we do is fresh and new and at the same time true to who the characters are."

And who is that in Ross's case? "Ross has a political bent similar to my own," Schwimmer muses. "He's kind of a conservative liberal in that he's open enough to accept a gay relationship between his ex-wife and her lover. But he's also a traditionalist in that he believes in family values – you know, man and wife and family – and working hard all your life." As complex and contradictory as these qualities are, Schwimmer wants even more from his character. "I've thought a lot about this," he says, "and what I've realized is that just as I have changed radically in the last several years, it's inevitable that Ross would

Rachel finally found out what millions of girls had known for an entire season. What took her so long?

too. It's almost as if I've experienced a loss of innocence in my own life – in a personal relationship, in the backlash of publicity we experienced as a cast, and in some business dealings – and it ended up informing my playing of Ross."

By the end of *Friends'* third season, Ross will be single and his whole life will have changed – not necessarily for the better. "He's been hurt and it will harden him to a degree," Schwimmer predicts. "He'll be cocky and a little less likable. But that's what I want for him. I'm constantly asking the writers to uncover other layers in Ross's personality. I love it that he's arrogant and competitive at times. The more complex he is, the more real I can make him."

Schwimmer is acutely aware of how indelible the role of Ross has been stamped in the public

Ross tends to dress the part of a tweedy scientist-type.

Costume design by Debra McGuire

mind and how closely he is identified with it. "People come up to me on the street and say 'Promise me you won't leave the show.' I'm like, 'I'm not going anywhere!'" Even so, he has no intention of staying locked inside of Ross, adorable and adored as he may be. "I did a series with Henry Winkler several years ago and I saw first hand how hard it was for him to be accepted as anything other than the Fonz. He was comfortable with it, but that's not me. Not that it's not wonderful to create a role that people remember for thirty years. But ultimately, you've got to make choices as you go along that will ensure that you'll be able to continue to work."

To make sure he makes the right choices, Schwimmer relies on the often painfully candid opinions of the members of his theater company. For instance, the general consensus among his support group was that his first big screen starring role in *The Pallbearer* was too similar to Ross. "I was perplexed by that," he says now. "I thought I'd done my homework." But Schwimmer, who has four very different films coming out in 1998, has been careful not to make the same mistake again. "In one of them,

Who's more compulsive ... Monica or Ross?

Kissing a Fool," he notes, "I play a character that is an insensitive, womanizing dog. He's the exact opposite of Ross. And believe me, it was absolutely intentional."

Because David Schwimmer's first love is the theater, it's not surprising that he says that working in front of a studio audience has given him the biggest thrill in doing the show. "With live theater you have the feeling of the audience being with you," he says, "and with *Friends* you have an audience that has been with you for *three years*! Like, when we were shooting Ross and Rachel's break-up – to feel the studio audience there with you – knowing what was at stake between the characters ... I've never experienced anything like it. It was so overwhelming that when it was over, and both of us were crying, it took a long time for me to get my bearings I was so shaken." Thanks to David Schwimmer, millions of viewers felt the same way. No matter what direction he takes in the coming years, they'll be there for him.

DAVID SCHWIMMER

FEATURE FILMS:

TWENTY BUCKS - Big Tomorrow Productions - Dir: Keeva Rosenfeld
CROSSING THE BRIDGE - Outlaw Productions - Dir: Mike Binder

TELEVISION:

MONTY - FOX - **Series Regular**

NYPD BLUE - ABC - **Recurring Role**
LA LAW - NBC - **Recurring Role**
THE WONDER YEARS - **Recurring Role**
WALTER AND EMILY - NBC

STAGE:

WEST	Mike	Lookingglass Theatre Company
THE ODYSSEY	Cyclops	Lookingglass Theatre Company
OF ONE BLOOD	Michael S.	Lookingglass Theatre Company
J.B.	J.B.	Northwestern University
RIMERS OF ELDRITCH	Skelly	Northwestern University
OH DAD, POOR DAD	Jonathan	Northwestern University
PRIVATE WARS	Natwick	Northwestern University
THE FROG PRINCE	Prince	Northwestern University

DIRECTING:

THE JUNGLE   *Winner of 6 Joseph Awards, Chicago
THE SERPENT By Jean Claude van Itallie
ALICE IN WONDERLAND *Toured the Edinburgh Festival, Scotland

TRAINING:

Frank Galati, Northwestern University (adaptation, directing)
David Downs, Northwestern University (acting, directing)
Rosemary Harris, B.A.D.A. at Oxford University (acting)

**"I feel a little older than the others," David Schwimmer says,
"with a little more perspective on things."**

The Dollhouse

Director:
Terry Hughes

Writers:
Wil Calhoun

Monica and Phoebe fight over their toys, and Chandler tries to break himself of the "I'll-Call-You" habit and Joey gets a taste of his own (bad) medicine.

ROSS HAS SOME SAD NEWS FOR Monica … their Aunt Sylvia has died. But Monica is thrilled because she's going to inherit Aunt Sylvia's beautiful Victorian dollhouse. Aunt Sylvia, mean rotten cruel bitch that she was, would never let little Monica play with her dollhouse while she was alive. Nooooo … it was only to be looked at, not played with. What a coincidence, Chandler says, his mother used to say the exact same thing to him. Phoebe says that she only had a barrel to play with when she was little. Monica promises Phoebe that she can come over and play with her new dollhouse any time she pleases.

And that's just what Phoebe does, bringing along a bag full of bizarre toys – a giant plastic dog,

> **"Well, maybe the dog's so big because the house was built on radioactive waste."**
>
> – *Phoebe* –

a tissue that's supposed to be a ghost, and a tiny dinosaur that barks. "I don't want a ghost," Monica growls. "Well, nobody *wants* a ghost," Phoebe points out. Monica turns into mean old Aunt Sylvia and bans Phoebe's rag-tag toys from the dollhouse. "Come," Phoebe orders them, "we're not welcome in the House of No Imagination." As she gets up to leave, Ross informs her that by the way, dinosaurs don't bark. But Phoebe says that yuh-huh … the little ones do.

A few days later, Phoebe shows up with an outrageously tacky second-hand dollhouse that has furniture made out of candy and a niche with a candle that she has christened "the aroma room."

It's so ridiculous that everyone wants to play with it, which, of course, makes Monica jealous. But that night the candle in the aroma room starts smoking and Phoebe's dollhouse catches fire. Ross puts it out in Monica's shower (with Monica in it).

Joey has gotten the lead in a very bad play. He's dazzled his leading lady, the very beautiful Kate, but she is hung up on the play's crackpot director. Lauren, Kate's perky blonde understudy, is in awe of Joey, who she always watched on *Days of Our Lives*. When Kate overhears the two of them make a date, she suddenly gets the hots for Joey and they end up in bed. Joey is blissed. Lauren is crushed. But the next day, Kate informs him that nothing has changed between them. What's the deal, he demands. He knows last night meant something to her. She's not *that* good an actress. She replies that she was just caught up in the Moment.

Chandler is a hit with Joanna, Rachel's bossy boss and Rachel asks him if he's interested. He says, yeah, sure, she seemed cool enough. But Joanna turns out to be, in Chandler's words, A BIG DULL DUD! Joanna, on the other hand, is positive that she and Chandler clicked like crazy. She tells her assistant to put him right through when he calls. And she knows he will, because he said he would. But of course, he doesn't. Rachel suggests that he might feel a little awkward because she's her boss. Joanna says pointedly that Rachel is the one who should be concerned about that.

Rachel insists that Chandler take Joanna out and tell her how he feels. And what is it with you guys and the always-saying-you'll-call-thing anyway, she wants to know. Chandler says that it's like this compulsive thing. And anyway, Joanna's not only dull but she gets this gross mascara glob in the corner of her eye.

Chandler does take Joanna to lunch a few days later. And as they're saying goodbye, he leaves her with handshake and a hearty "Take Care," but then,

he suddenly blurts out, "This was great. I'll give you a call some time." But Rachel pulls him back. "I'm not going to call you." He admits sheepishly, "I'm sorry I said I was going to when I'm not. This has nothing to do with you. I have issues with commitment, intimacy … mascara goop." Joanna says she appreciates his honesty, and Chandler is massively relieved. So relieved, he ends up saying, "This was great. I'll give you a call."

Phoebe's dollhouse is ever so much more fun than Monica's House of No Imagination.

How could Rachel have known that Chandler would think Joanna was a BIG DULL DUD when she set them up?

(Far left) **The highfalutin' Kate will decide she's interested in Joey as soon as she realizes that …** (left) **he's interested in her understudy, Lauren.**

The Chick And A Duck

Director:
Michael Lembeck

Writer:
Chris Brown

Ross foregoes his TV debut to look after the injured Rachel;
Pete buys Monica her own restaurant; and Chandler and Joey
fall in love with an Easter chick.

MONICA CRASHES INTO RACHEL WHILE PRACTISING ON the roller skates she's supposed to wear for work. The pain gets worse as the day wears on, but there's nothing Rachel can do since she's expected for dinner at her boss's house that night. She asks Ross to help her get ready – which he does, not bothering to tell her he's scheduled to make an appearance on the Discovery Channel in just a few hours himself.

After applying her make-up (à la Ann Margaret ca. 1972) he then tries to help her get into her clothes. When she's suddenly shy, he reminds her that he's seen her naked hundreds of times and that all he has to do is close his eyes to see her that way anytime. As she lifts her arm, she cries out in pain signaling Ross that the injury is more serious than she'd originally let on. He insists she go to the

hospital and heads downstairs to get her a cab. "You're not going with me?" she asks. Of course he is. He's just got to make a call.

Chandler becomes the primary caregiver to an Easter chick Joey brings home, naming it "Little Yasmine," after his *Baywatch* dream girl, Yasmine Bleeth. But he snaps one night after Joey announces that he's going out for the umpteenth time. "I'm stuck here all day and you come in and spend two seconds with us," he rails, "and then you expect to go off gallivanting with your friends?" It's obvious that Joey and Chandler weren't ready to have a chick. They decide to give it back.

Pete tells Monica he's bought her a restaurant – her dream ever since she got her first Easy Bake Oven. But how can she accept his offer, knowing that he's still hung up on her? Pete assures her that

Chandler wonders if Little Yasmine can swim as well as his new duck.

those days are over. In fact, he's met somebody else. Monica is ecstatic. Now she can work for him with a clear conscience. After she skates off to give notice at the diner, Phoebe, who's been eavesdropping on this exchange, busts Pete: "This woman, she's fictitious, no?" she asks. Phoebe's right: she's fictitious, yes.

Monica is overcome with paroxysms of joy at the sight of the new restaurant's ultra-equipped kitchen. But she's still concerned about Pete's feelings. "Look," he says, "I'm the one who stands to get hurt here and I can handle that." The problem is she can't. Impulsively, he pulls her close and kisses her. "I'm sorry …" he begins. "Shut up for a second," she says, and kisses him back. "Oh wow," she says and she kisses him again.

Joey is surprised to see the chick still in the apartment when he gets home the next night. Chandler tells him that the shelter said if they couldn't find her a home, they would have to kill it. No way was he going to let that happen to Little Yasmine. Joey is totally supportive until a duck waddles out of Chandler's bedroom. "Funny story …" Chandler begins.

Later that evening Chandler is in the hall disciplining the duck – which had evidently gotten too chummy with Little Yasmine – when Ross and Rachel return from the hospital. "How'd it go tonight?" he asks Ross. How did *what* go, Rachel asks. Oh, nothing, Ross answers. After getting her settled, he admits that he was "kinda supposed to be on TV tonight." But why didn't he say anything, she demands to know. "Because I knew if I told you, you'd make me go," he replies. Rachel is beyond touched. They both look at each other for what seems like a very long time.

TO: Todd

BENAY'S
BIRD & ANIMAL SOURCE

Date: 3/7/97   Invoice No. WBF 9418

Production Co.: Warner Bros.   Product: Friends
The One w/ the Chick & the Duck

P.O. Number:

Job Number:

Phone:

ANIMALS

10 Baby Chicks
10 Baby Ducks
4 Adult white Ducks $ x

5 frozen chickens
15 additional Baby Chicks
Transportation $ x 5 days
2/3 trainers on timecard

Total Now Due $

"We had a bathtub duck and a walking duck. The walking duck was like a character actor — he always did funny stuff with his tail that made us laugh. We also had a stuffed chick that we used as a chick double. For the part where Chandler puts the chick in the tub to see if it can swim, we dammed up the tub and put it in a pail. There was duck cam and chick cam and we just kept rolling so we always had plenty of stuff."

Michael Lembeck

The Screamer

Director: **Peter Bonerz**

Writers: **Shana Goldberg-Meehan & Scott Silveri**

Joey finds (then loses) his first real love and no one believes Ross when he insists that Rachel is dating a psycho.

WHAT ARE YOU, A MORON, HUH? The Screamer (guest star Ben Stiller) tactfully informs an unwitting couple that they're sitting in his seats. Director Peter Bonerz (bottom, second from left) **also guest stars.**

JOEY'S NEW PLAY IS OPENING TONIGHT, AND HE WANTS to make sure everyone has a ticket. Monica says she'll need two for her and her boyfriend. (She likes the way that sounds.) Rachel, Chandler, and Phoebe all say they'll just need one. Ross, however, is going to need two because he'll be bringing a date – that is if Rachel doesn't mind. Rachel doesn't mind at all, she says, in fact, she's bringing a date too. Now Joey's confused. He thought she said one. No, Rachel explains that was me *plus* one. So, does that mean that Chandler and Phoebe also need two?

At the theater that night, Ross is dumbfounded when Rachel's date Tommy (guest star Ben Stiller) has a hysterical fit when he finds a couple sitting in their seats. "WHAT ARE YOU, A MORON, HUH?" he screams at the cowering pair. "The usher said these were our seats," the man (director and guest star Peter Bonerz) begins... "OH, THE USHER MUST BE RIGHT," Tommy yells, "WHAT WITH ALL THE TRAINING THEY GO THROUGH. *GET OUT!*" This guy is obviously demented. But how is Ross going to tell Rachel?

At the party after the play, the director reads the review out loud, "Joey Tribbiani gives an uneven performance, but Mr. Tribbiani is not the worst thing in this production." *All right*! Joey shouts. That's his best review to date. The director goes on to Joey's co-star, "Kate Miller's awkward and

Kate is leaving on a jet plane for the coast, but she takes a second to stop and say goodbye to Joey. (Maybe she feels something for him after all.)

mannered portrayal is laughable." Kate is crushed, but not as much as the director who screams at the celebrants: "Thank you boys and girls for ruining my life! Please stuff your talentless faces with my mother's crab cakes." After he takes her home, Joey tries to console Kate, assuring her that the critics are jealous because she's just so darn talented and good-looking. She feels better now and, to his surprise, starts to nuzzle him. "I don't get you," he tells her, "first you hate me, then you sleep with me, then you have nothing to do with me. Now you want me again?" "What's the matter," she says, "haven't you ever dated an actress before?" But before he can answer, she passes out. Joey is still with her when she wakes up later. They end up talking till daybreak – a first for both of them.

Later at Central Perk, Ross tells Rachel she shouldn't see Tommy anymore, that he's just plain mean. Assuming he's jealous, the gang gives him a hard time. As he stalks out mumbling to himself, he – literally – runs into Tommy and spills coffee on his shirt. "WHAT ARE YOU, JUST A BIG DUMB IDIOT WITH A BIG DUMB IDIOT HAIRDO?" Tommy screams. Ross tries to get the gang's attention by tapping on the window, but no one hears the tirade. Ultimately though Ross is vindicated when Tommy blows his cover by screaming at Joey and Chandler's baby chick after it piddles on his hand. "YOU IDIOT," he yells at the little fuzzy creature. "YOU'RE SO STUPID, HOW ARE YOU NOT EXTINCT?" Next he turns his rancor on the duck

which has waddled out of the bedroom. "WHAT ARE YOU QUACKING ABOUT, YOU DUMB DONALD DO-DO?" Pausing for a second, he sees Chandler, Monica, Joey and Rachel standing in the doorway watching him. "I guess we're not going out anymore," he jeers at Rachel as he strides past her and, with any luck, out of her life.

When Joey makes his entrance in the play that night, he's startled to find Kate's understudy, Lauren, playing her part. During a break, Joey finds Kate waiting for him backstage. She tells him she's gotten a part on *General Hospital* and she's leaving for L.A. tonight. Looking back at her as she stands in the wings, Joey delivers his final speech with an uncharacteristic fire. Kate blows him a kiss and slips away.

"I guess we're not going out anymore," Tommy says to Rachel. (He guesses right.)

THE ONE WITH
Ross's Thing

Director:
Shelley Jensen

Writers:

**Andrew Reich
& Ted Cohen**

Phoebe acts as shallow as any guy by dating two men at once; Monica thinks Pete might propose; and Ross does battle with a little thing on his behind that just won't go away.

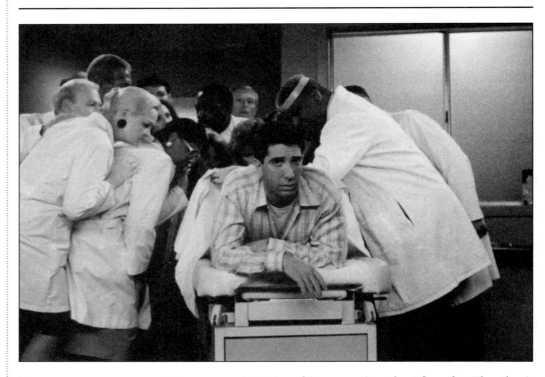

The doctors have never seen anything like Ross's Thing.

ROSS ASKS A LITTLE FAVOR FROM CHANDLER AND JOEY. Actually, it's a big favor considering who they are. It seems he's found this little, uh, thing on a part of his body that's not visually accessible to him and he wants them to tell him what it is. Joey says it's too wrinkly to be a mole. And Chandler says it's fancier than a pimple. And that, pretty much, is the extent of the enlightenment they have to offer.

Ross has no choice but to take The Thing to a real doctor. But even the doctor doesn't know what it is. He calls in some associates to check it out and they call in a few more and, before long, the entire hospital – or so it seems – has come to gawk at ... well, whatever it is.

Meanwhile, Phoebe has never been happier. She's on a roll – dating two guys at the same time. One is Vince, a hunky fireman who has 98 hot saves

and is super serious about fire safety. The other is Jason, a kind-hearted kindergarten teacher who isn't so bad either. Wow, is she having fun playing the field! Or anyway, she is until she starts to feel like she's working in the field rather than playing it. She's constantly afraid one of them is going to catch her with the other. But how can she possibly decide between the two? Vince is a guy-guy. Translation: he's "burly." But Jason has something really sweet and rare; he's sensitive. Burly versus sensitive. It's a tough call.

Monica, on the other hand, is sure that Pete wants to break up with her. She – and the gang – go to his apartment so they can "talk" on his video-phone. But Pete only says that he loves her and he'll tell her more when he sees her. Then, while snooping around, Joey finds a check made out to Hugo

Lindgren Ring Design. Rachel is sure Pete is going to propose.

Phoebe has made her choice. It's Jason ... Mr. Sensitive. She goes to the firehouse to break things off with Vince but he's so upset, he rushes off to write in his journal. Uh-oh. Vince is sensitive, as well as being burly.

Okay, so Jason is out. At least that's the plan until Phoebe happens to see him without his shirt. And, wouldn't you know it – he, too, is burly. Now what's she supposed to do?

Ross has given up on doctors and gone to see Phoebe's fruitcake herbalist, Guru Saj. Miracle of miracles, Guru Saj actually knows what Ross's thing is. It's a coundis. He puts a salve on it, but that appears to anger it. Guru Saj says he must resort to a stronger medicine ... love. As he spreads love with big circular motions, he happens to catch the coundis on his watch.

Monica has decided that she might actually say yes, if Pete asks the Big Question. But Pete's news is that he wants to become the world's Ultimate Fighting champ. In fact, he's even designed his own octagon-shaped ring. And he wants her with him when he wins – close enough to smell the blood.

> **"I'm playing the field. I'm juggling two guys. I'm sowing my wild oats. I'm like some kind of oat-sowing, field-playing juggler."**
>
> *– Phoebe –*

A week or so later Vince is watching Phoebe sing one of her own compositions called "Crazy Underwear (creeping up my butt)." But then, the inevitable happens when Jason walks in and kisses her (on the lips). "Hey," Vince barks, "what's going on here?" Jason ends up storming out when he hears that Phoebe has slept with Vince and Vince does the same after hearing that Phoebe made Jason a candlelit dinner in the park. There's no way he can possibly be serious about someone who lit a fire in a wooded area.

Phoebe started out playing the field, but now she's beginning to feel like she's *working* the field.

The Ultimate Fighting Champion

Director:
Robby Benson

Story:
**Mark Kunerth &
Pang-Ni Landrum**

Teleplay:
**Scott Silveri &
Shana Goldberg-
Meehan**

Pete continues to pursue his dream of becoming the Ultimate Fighting Champ even though it may mean losing Monica, and Chandler tries to sidestep an overly friendly boss.

THIS IS THE ONE WITH THE ULTIMATE FIGHTING Champion, but it's also the one where two guys wander into Central Perk and have an extremely gross conversation about their wives and their gynaecologists and who's doing what to the other. And then they get all huffy when the gang eavesdrops! They don't seem to know that they're sitting on the Friends' sofa, but in all fairness, the Friends don't seem to notice that the two guys are Billy Crystal and Robin Williams either.

But back to important stuff. Pete is still into this Ultimate Fighting fixation and Monica is not happy. For one thing, she knows how dangerous it is since Chandler and Joey described it to her in gory eye-gouging, butt-kicking detail. And now, Hoshi, Pete's trainer, has forbidden any "boomboom" before the fight.

On a slightly less life-threatening note, Phoebe has asked Rachel if she can fix Ross up with her girlfriend Bonnie. Now Rachel shouldn't care, and she doesn't, once she confirms that this Bonnie is the person she thinks she is – a weird girl with a bald head. But then, Bonnie shows up at Central Perk and not only has her hair grown out, but it's long and blonde. (And she's a babe.)

Ross and Bonnie hit it off immediately. "This is all your fault," Rachel hisses at Phoebe . "We've got to break them up." But Phoebe doesn't get it. "Aren't you the one who doesn't want to be with Ross? Don't you want him to be happy?" Rachel says yes and yes she does, but not this happy, this soon.

And then there's Chandler whose macho boss has taken to rewarding him for a good job or even a good line, with an enthusiastic whack on the butt. Joey thinks maybe this is just a jock thing. No reason to make a stink. But the girls, who know this kind of squirrelly routine all too well, think that's exactly what Chandler should do. They urge him to

The gang watch in horror as Pete gets massacred in the Ultimate Fighting Championships.

rub something smelly on his behind. But Chandler takes a slightly more subtle approach, suggesting to the boss that all the, uh, special attention he's been getting is making the other guys in the office jealous. Not only does the boss buy it, he loves him even more. So much, it's all he can do to keep from giving him another smack.

On the night of Pete's first fight, he looks ready to rumble as he makes his splashy entrance into the arena. He's got Monica – literally – in his corner and she's behind him all the way. That is, until she catches sight of his opponent – one Tank Abbott, a 300-pound street brawler. "Don't do it," she pleads. But it's too late. The bell rings and Tank hoists Pete and spins him gleefully overhead. Afterwards, Monica hugs the battered warrior and tells him how proud she is that he went the distance. So he can stop now, right? But Pete is not going to give up until he is the Ultimate Fighting Champ of the World. Oh, and nothing personal, but Hoshi has barred her from ringside. Something about her blowing his concentration.

Pete's next fight is even shorter than the last. At the hospital the next day, Monica gives him an ultimatum: "I care about you too much to see you hurt yourself this way." Determined to take a stand,

> "We always knew we wanted Monica to get involved with a billionaire genius scientist whom she wasn't physically attracted to in any way. But it was a very tough casting thing because you had to have someone who was appealing enough that we like him, so we can root for him, but on the other hand, isn't so drop-dead male model gorgeous that we would go 'what's your problem?' to Monica when she didn't fall for him. I always had a Bill Gates image in my head till we saw John Favreau – who is just a really good actor and a very appealing guy."
>
> DAVID CRANE

she turns to leave. But maybe all is not lost. "Can you leave me a note?" Pete asks, "'Cause I'm on a lot of painkillers and I don't know whether I'll remember this tomorrow."

In the meantime, Chandler's boss has now taken to smacking everyone but him. Naturally, this makes him feel like a loser. "Are you feeling left out?" the boss asks him. Chandler nods sheepishly.

(Above) **Ross is definitely interested in Bonnie, but then again, he's never seen her with her shaved head.**
(Below) **Who's gonna protect who here? Ross goes along to look after Monica as Pete competes in an Ultimate Fighting match.**

The Beach

Director: **Pamela Fryman**
Story: **Pang-Ni Landrum & Mark Kunerth**
Teleplay: **Adam Chase**

Ross and Rachel realize that they're not completely over each other and Phoebe discovers that her Mom's best friend is actually her real mother.

THE WHOLE GANG HEADS OUT TO THE BEACH TO SPEND the weekend at the house of Phoebe's client with the fuzzy back. While she's there, Phoebe intends to look up her mother's BFF ("Best Friend Forever") from high school, whose name also happens to be Phoebe, in the hope that she'll tell her some stories about her mom and real dad.

Naturally it rains and the house floods, and the guys have no choice but to stay inside. Joey campaigns vigorously for a game of strip poker – or strip anything, actually. They settle on an updated version of the Happy Days Game – wherein 5 "Cool Points" allow a player to divest another of a piece of clothing. Several pitchers of margaritas help to get the game in gear. Hours later it turns out that the gang has pooled their Cool Points to divest Joey of his clothes. But even more interestingly, something is definitely sparking between Ross and Rachel.

But then Ross's new girlfriend Bonnie arrives. And she and Ross have such a noisy night together that Chandler swears the racket made sea turtles come up to the house.

Phoebe shows up unannounced at the house of her namesake (guest star Teri Garr) and starts showering her with questions about her parents.

"They had a special name for your mother and father and me in high school ... 'The Three Losers.'"
– *Big Phoebe*

"Well, we were always together," Big Phoebe remembers. "In fact, the other kids had a nickname for us ... 'The Three Losers.'" She then observes sadly that her mother's suicide must have been very hard for her. "Yeah, no, it was great," Little Phoebe says in that special way of hers. Whatever, they make a date to talk more tomorrow.

"I just gotta tell you," Rachel says to Bonnie the next day, "I just loved your look when you were bald." Bonnie is flattered and mentions that's she's been thinking of shaving her head again. Rachel urges to go for it ... like, now.

Ross's reaction to Bonnie's new G.I. Jane look is a definite Yuck. Later when he accuses Rachel of instigating the billiard ball haircut, she insists that she only gave her a little nudge in that direction. "No," says Ross, "you gave her the *razor*." Eventually Rachel admits that maybe she did it because she still has feelings for him. They kiss until Joey and Chandler interrupt them. Rachel announces that she's going upstairs, and looks back longingly at Ross as she walks away.

When Big Phoebe suddenly flakes out on their date, Phoebe sneaks into her house in the middle of the night to search for information on her parents. She's looking through a stack of papers when Big Phoebe almost beans her with a wooden hanger. "What are you doing here?" she shrieks. "I deserve to know where I came from," Little Phoebe answers tremulously, "so if you can help me find my father then you should. Otherwise you're just mean." Big Phoebe acknowledges that she's right and that's why she's got to tell her the truth: *she is her mother!*

Back at the beach house, Ross is agonizing over Rachel to Chandler and Joey: "If I go up there and kiss her and it doesn't work out ..." Joey is interested in knowing if any of this means that Bonnie will be free tonight.

Ross slowly makes his way up the stairs. He pauses at Bonnie's door, then at Rachel's. Finally, he opens one and steps inside.

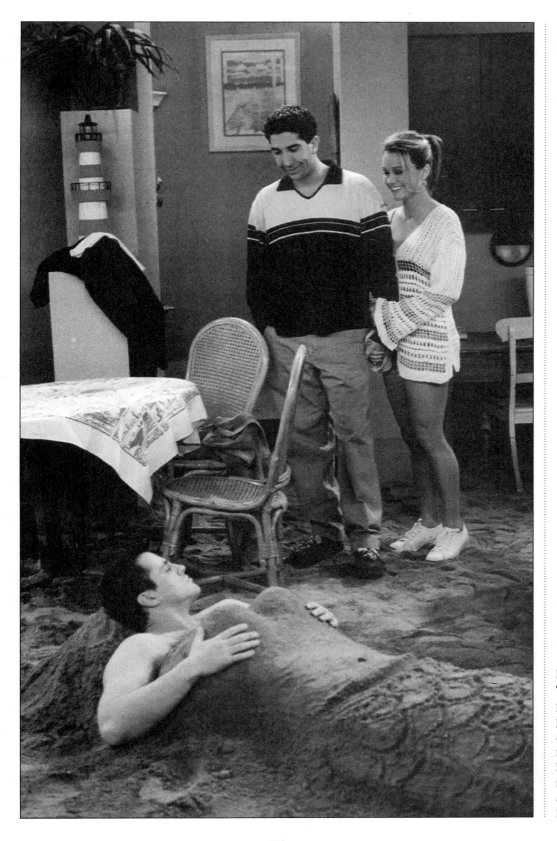

He's a merman! The gang played a little joke on Joey after he fell into a deep Marguerita-induced sleep at the beach house.